# 101 Labs
# Linux LPIC-1

*Includes Linux Essentials*

**WITHDRAWN**

Wellesley Free Library

**Paul Browning**, LLB (Hons), CCNP, MCSE
**Arturo Norberto Baldo**

This study guide and/or material is not sponsored by, endorsed by or affiliated with The Linux Professional Institute Inc. Linux, LPIC1 and Ubuntu are trademarks or registered trademarks of Linus Torvalds, Linux Professional Institute Inc. and Canonical Ltd. in the United States and certain other countries. All other trademarks are trademarks of their respective owners.

101 Labs is a registered trademark.

COPYRIGHT NOTICE

Copyright 2019 Paul Browning, all rights reserved. No portion of this book may be reproduced mechanically, electronically, or by any other means, including photocopying without written permission of the publisher.

https://www.101labs.net

ISBN: 978-0-9928239-1-7

Published by Reality Press Ltd.

LEGAL NOTICE

The advice in this book is designed to help you achieve the standard of LPIC-1: System Administrator. The LPIC-1 will validate the candidate's ability to perform maintenance tasks on the command line, install and configure a computer running Linux and configure basic networking. Before you carry out more complex operations, it is advisable to seek the advice of experts.

The practical scenarios in this book are meant only to illustrate a technical point and should be used only on your privately owned equipment and never on a live network.

# About the Authors

## *Paul Browning*

Paul Browning worked as a police officer in the UK for 12 years before changing careers and becoming a helpdesk technician. He passed several IT certifications and began working for Cisco Systems doing WAN support for large enterprise customers.

He started an IT consulting company in 2002 and helped to design, install, configure, and troubleshoot global networks for small to large companies. He started teaching IT courses soon after that and through his classroom courses, online training, and study guides has helped tens of thousands of people pass their IT exams and enjoy successful careers in the IT industry.

In 2006 Paul started the online IT training portal www.howtonetwork.com, which has grown to become one of the leading IT certification websites.

In 2013 Paul moved to Brisbane with his family. In his spare time he plays the guitar, reads, drinks coffee, and practices Brazilian jiu-jitsu.

## *Arturo Norberto Baldo*

Arturo Norberto Baldo did the technical edit on this book. He is a Linux enthusiast, network engineer at AS26218 and has been a freelance IT consultant since 2012, ISOC and IETF member. He holds too many certifications to list here. He supports technologies including VMware ESXi, Vcenter, Veeam Backup And Replication, Spiceworks, osTicket, Active Directory, Windows Servers, Debian and Ubuntu Servers, Web Hosting Panels, Video surveillance systems: Bosch BVMS, Genetec, Digifort and Mileston and others.

He has worked as a network engineer, systems administrator and security specialist for several large companies. He holds a Bachelor of Technology (B.Tech.) and Master of Technology (M.Tech.). He likes to read and cycle in his spare time.

# Table of Contents

**Introduction–101 Labs** .................................................................................................. ix
**LPI–Linux Essentials** ..................................................................................................... 1
    Lab 1    Linux Evolution and Popular Operating Systems ................................................ 3
    Lab 2    Major Open Source Applications: Desktop ......................................................... 5
    Lab 3    Major Open Source Applications: Server ............................................................ 9
    Lab 4    Open Source Software and Licensing ................................................................ 13
    Lab 5    ICT Skills and Working in Linux ........................................................................ 15
    Lab 6    Command Line Basics: Syntax and Quoting ..................................................... 17
    Lab 7    Command Line Basics: Environment Variables, Types, and History ............... 19
    Lab 8    Using the Command Line to Get Help ............................................................... 21
    Lab 9    Using Directories and Listing Files: Files .......................................................... 23
    Lab 10   Using Directories and Listing Files: Directories ............................................... 25
    Lab 11   Creating, Moving, and Deleting Files ................................................................ 27
    Lab 12   Archiving Files on the Command Line .............................................................. 31
    Lab 13   Searching and Extracting Data from Files: Pipes and Redirection ................... 35
    Lab 14   Searching and Extracting Data from Files: Regular Expressions ...................... 39
    Lab 15   Turning Commands into a Script: Shell Scripting ............................................ 41
    Lab 16   Turning Commands into a Script: Scripting Practice ....................................... 43
    Lab 17   Choosing an Operating System .......................................................................... 45
    Lab 18   Understanding Computer Hardware .................................................................. 47
    Lab 19   Where Data is Stored: Processes and Configuration ......................................... 49
    Lab 20   Where Data is Stored: System Messaging and Logging .................................... 51
    Lab 21   Your Computer on the Network ........................................................................ 53
    Lab 22   Basic Security and Identifying User Types ....................................................... 55
    Lab 23   Creating Users and Groups ................................................................................ 59
    Lab 24   Managing File Permissions and Ownership ...................................................... 61
    Lab 25   Special Directories and Files .............................................................................. 63
**LPIC1 Linux Administrator–Exam 101** ...................................................................... 65
    Lab 26   Determine and Configure Hardware Settings: PCI Devices and Peripherals ... 67
    Lab 27   Determine and Configure Hardware Settings: Filesystems and Storage .......... 69
    Lab 28   Boot the System: Boot Sequence ....................................................................... 71

| Lab 29 | Boot the System: SysVInit and Systemd | 75 |
| --- | --- | --- |
| Lab 30 | Change Runlevels / Boot Targets and Shutdown or Reboot System: Runlevels and Boot Targets | 77 |
| Lab 31 | Change Runlevels / Boot Targets and Shutdown or Reboot System: Systemd and Processes | 79 |
| Lab 32 | Design Hard Disk Layout | 81 |
| Lab 33 | Install a Boot Manager | 83 |
| Lab 34 | Manage Shared Libraries | 85 |
| Lab 35 | Use Debian Package Management: Apt | 87 |
| Lab 36 | Use Debian Package Management: Dpkg | 89 |
| Lab 37 | Use RPM and YUM Package Management: YUM | 91 |
| Lab 38 | Use RPM and YUM Package Management: RPM | 93 |
| Lab 39 | Linux as a Virtualization Guest | 95 |
| Lab 40 | Work on the Command Line: Commands and Quoting | 97 |
| Lab 41 | Work on the Command Line: Environment Variables, Types, and History | 101 |
| Lab 42 | Process Text Streams Using Filters | 103 |
| Lab 43 | Perform Basic File Management: Files and Directories | 107 |
| Lab 44 | Perform Basic File Management: Find and Globbing | 111 |
| Lab 45 | Perform Basic File Management: Archiving and Unarchiving | 113 |
| Lab 46 | Use Streams, Pipes, and Redirects: Redirection and File Descriptors | 117 |
| Lab 47 | Use Streams, Pipes, and Redirects: Pipes | 121 |
| Lab 48 | Create, Monitor, and Kill Processes: Foreground and Background Jobs | 123 |
| Lab 49 | Create, Monitor, and Kill Processes: Process Monitoring | 127 |
| Lab 50 | Create, Monitor, and Kill Processes: Sending Signals | 129 |
| Lab 51 | Modify Process Execution Priorities | 131 |
| Lab 52 | Search Text Files Using Regular Expressions: Basic Regex | 133 |
| Lab 53 | Search Text Files Using Regular Expressions: Extended Regex | 137 |
| Lab 54 | Basic File Editing: vi Navigation | 141 |
| Lab 55 | Basic File Editing: vi Modes | 143 |
| Lab 56 | Create Partitions and Filesystems | 145 |
| Lab 57 | Maintain the Integrity of Filesystems | 147 |
| Lab 58 | Control Mounting and Unmounting of Filesystems: Manual Mounting | 151 |
| Lab 59 | Control Mounting and Unmounting of Filesystems: Automatic Mounting | 153 |
| Lab 60 | Manage File Permissions and Ownership: File Permissions | 155 |
| Lab 61 | Manage File Permissions and Ownership: Directory Permissions | 159 |
| Lab 62 | Create and Change Hard and Symbolic Links | 163 |
| Lab 63 | Find System Files and Place Files in the Correct Location | 165 |

**LPIC1 Linux Administrator–Exam 102** .................................................................. 167
   Lab 64  Customize and Use the Shell Environment: User Profiles ................... 169
   Lab 65  Customize and Use the Shell Environment: Aliases and Functions ...... 171
   Lab 66  Customize or Write Simple Scripts: Standard Syntax .......................... 173
   Lab 67  Customize or Write Simple Scripts: Miscellaneous Tools ..................... 175
   Lab 68  Customize or Write Simple Scripts: Scripting Practice ......................... 177
   Lab 69  Install and Configure X11 ........................................................................ 179
   Lab 70  Graphical Desktops .................................................................................. 181
   Lab 71  Accessibility ............................................................................................... 183
   Lab 72  Manage User and Group Accounts and Related System Files: Users .... 185
   Lab 73  Manage User and Group Accounts and Related System Files: Groups ... 189
   Lab 74  Manage User and Group Accounts and Related System Files: Special
            Purpose Accounts .................................................................................... 191
   Lab 75  Automate System Administration Tasks by Scheduling Jobs: Cron ....... 193
   Lab 76  Automate System Administration Tasks by Scheduling Jobs:
            At and Systemd ........................................................................................ 195
   Lab 77  Localization and Internationalization: Timezones ................................ 197
   Lab 78  Localisation and Internationalisation: Locales ....................................... 199
   Lab 79  Maintain System Time: NTP .................................................................. 201
   Lab 80  Maintain System Time: Chrony .............................................................. 203
   Lab 81  System Logging: Rsyslog .......................................................................... 205
   Lab 82  System Logging: Logrotate ...................................................................... 207
   Lab 83  System Logging: Journald ........................................................................ 209
   Lab 84  Mail Transfer Agent (MTA) Basics: Aliases and Forwarding ............... 211
   Lab 85  Mail Transfer Agent (MTA) Basics: Other MTA's .................................. 215
   Lab 86  Manage Printers and Printing ................................................................. 217
   Lab 87  Fundamentals of Internet Protocols: Ports and Services ...................... 219
   Lab 88  Fundamentals of Internet Protocols: Subnetting ................................. 221
   Lab 89  Fundamentals of Internet Protocols: IPv4 and IPv6 ............................. 223
   Lab 90  Persistent Network Configuration: Network Configuration ............... 225
   Lab 91  Persistent Network Configuration: NetworkManager ........................ 227
   Lab 92  Basic Network Troubleshooting: Modern Tools ................................... 229
   Lab 93  Basic Network Troubleshooting: Legacy Tools ..................................... 231
   Lab 94  Configure Client-Side DNS: dnsutils ..................................................... 233
   Lab 95  Configure Client-Side DNS: systemd-resolved ..................................... 235
   Lab 96  Perform Security Administration Tasks: User Auditing ....................... 237
   Lab 97  Perform Security Administration Tasks: System Auditing ................... 239

Lab 98   Setup Host Security: User Security ............................................. 241
Lab 99   Setup Host Security: Network Services ....................................... 243
Lab 100  Securing Data with Encryption: SSH .......................................... 245
Lab 101  Securing Data with Encryption: GPG .......................................... 247

# Introduction–101 Labs

Welcome to your 101 Labs book.

When I started teaching IT courses back in 2002, I was shocked to discover that most training manuals were almost exclusively dedicated to theoretical knowledge. Apart from a few examples of commands to use or configuration guidelines, you were left to plough through without ever knowing how to apply what you learned to live equipment or to the real world.

Fast forward 17 years and little has changed. I still wonder how, when around 50% of your exam marks are based on hands-on skills and knowledge, most books give little or no regard to equipping you with the skills you need to both pass the exam and then make money in your chosen career as a network, security, or cloud engineer (or whichever career path you choose).

101 Labs is NOT a theory book: it's here to transform what you have learned in your study guides into valuable skills you will be using from day one on your job as a network engineer. We don't teach DHCP, for example; instead, we show you how to configure a DHCP server, which addresses you shouldn't use, and which parameters you can allocate to hosts. If the protocol isn't working, we show you what the probable cause is. Sound useful? We certainly hope so.

We choose the most relevant parts of the exam syllabus and use free software or free trials (whenever possible) to walk you through configuration and troubleshooting commands step by step. As your confidence grows, we increase the difficulty level. If you want to be an exceptional network engineer, you can make your own labs up, add other technologies, try to break them, fix them, and do it all over again.

–Paul Browning

# 101 LABS–LINUX LPIC-1: SYSTEM ADMINISTRATOR

This book is designed to cement the theory you have read in your Linux LPIC-1 study guide or video training course. If you haven't studied any theory yet, then please check out our website https://www.howtonetwork.com, which also features practice exams.

The goal of this book is to dramatically improve your hands-on skills and speed, enabling you to succeed in the practical portions of the Linux LPIC exams and also to transfer your skills to the real world as a Linux network engineer. We don't have space here to cover theory at all, so please refer to your Linux LPIC study guide to get a good understanding of the learning points behind each lab. Every lab is designed to cover a particular theoretical issue, such as the configuration requirements of fdisk.

If you want to become Linux LPIC-1 certified, you must pass two exams:

> 101-500 and
> 102-500

The book actually starts with the Linux Essentials syllabus for labs 1 through 25. If you wish to take this certification you can book the exam:

> 010-160

Please visit the LPIC website for information about the exam topics and booking details: https://www.lpi.org

We've done our best to hit every syllabus topic mentioned in the exam syllabus on the Linux Professional Institute website. Please do check the syllabus on their website which may change. Their website also gives more details on the weighting given each subject area.

It's also worth noting that once we show you how to configure a certain service or protocol a few times, we stop walking you through the steps in subsequent labs—to save valuable space. Anyway, you can always flick back a few pages to see how it's done.

We've done our best to keep the topology as simple as possible, for this reason, almost all labs have been configured on a Ubuntu installation running on a virtual machine (with internet access). Please do check out our resources page, which will cover any additional information you need: https://www.101labs.com/resources

## DOING THE LABS

Apart from a couple of research labs at the start, all of the labs are hands-on. They have been checked by several students as well as a senior Linux consultant so should be error-free. Bear in mind that each machine will differ so your output will differ from ours in many instances. If you use a distro other than Ubuntu 18.04 then your results will differ from ours significantly.

If you get stuck or things aren't working, we recommend you take a break and come back to the lab later with a clear mind. There are many Linux support forums out there where you can ask questions, and if you are a member of 101labs.net you can post on our forum, of course.

Best of luck with your studies.

–Paul Browning, CCNP, MCSE

## 101 LABS–LINUX LPIC1 VIDEO COURSE

Each 101 Labs book has an associated video training course. You can watch the instructor configure each lab and talk you through the entire process step by step as well as share helpful tips for the real world of IT. Each course also has 200 exam-style questions to prepare you for the real thing. It's certainly not necessary to take use this resource, but if you do, please use the coupon code '101lpic' at the checkout page to get a big discount as a thank you for buying this book. https://www.101labs.net

## INSTRUCTIONS

1. Please follow the labs from start to finish. If you get stuck, do the next lab and come back to the problem lab later. There is a good chance you will work out the solution as you gain confidence and experience in configuring the software and using the commands.
2. You can take the labs in any order, but we've done our best to build up your skill level as you go along. For best results, do ALL the labs several times over before attempting the exam.
3. There are resources at www.101labs.net/resources.
4. Please DO NOT configure these labs on a live network or on equipment belonging to private companies or individuals.

5. Please DO NOT attempt to configure these labs on other Linux distros. We've chosen Ubuntu (18.04 LTS ) for the labs due to the fact its the most popular Linux distribution among the top 1000 sites and gains around 500 of the top 10 million websites per day.
6. You MUST be reading or have read a Linux study guide or watched a theory video course. Apart from some configuration tips and suggestions, we don't explain much theory in this book; it's all hands-on labs.
7. It's impossible for us to give individual support to the thousands of readers of this book (sorry!), so please don't contact us for tech support. Each lab has been tested by several tech editors from beginner to expert.

## ALSO FROM REALITY PRESS LTD.

Cisco CCNA Simplified
Cisco CCNA in 60 Days
IP Subnetting—Zero to Guru
101 Labs—CompTIA A+ (due 2019)
101 Labs—CompTIA Network+
101 Labs—IP Subnetting
101 Labs—Cisco CCNP
101 Labs—Cisco CCNA
101 Labs—Wireshark WCNA (due 2019)

## TECHNICAL EDITORS

Thanks to all the tech editors who donated their time to check all the labs and give feedback.

Charles L. Burkholder
Carol Wood
Dante J. Alarcon
Timothy A Clark
Tim Peel
Elbert L Freeman
John DeGennaro
Steve Quan

# LPI–Linux Essentials

# LAB 1

# Linux Evolution and Popular Operating Systems

**Lab Objective:**
Understand what Linux is, how various Linux distributions evolved, and the use cases and target audiences of those distributions. Install Ubuntu 18.04, or a distro of your choice, into a VM.

**Lab Purpose:**
Unlike with proprietary operating systems, Linux's nature means that its users have limitless options in terms of what software will (and won't) be installed on their computers. There are hundreds of Linux distributions or "distros" available today, but Linux didn't begin that way. Debian, Slackware, and Red Hat have existed since the early 1990s and are three of the oldest distros still in use. Many of the current most popular distros were derived or forked from one of those three.

**Lab Tool:**
An internet-connected computer that can support VirtualBox, or another hypervisor software.

**Lab Topology:**
N/A

**Lab Walkthrough:**

*Task 1:*
Review this tree of Linux distributions (see URL in the notes). Try to locate some of the most commonly used distros:

- Debian
- Ubuntu
- CentOS
- SUSE
- Red Hat
- Linux Mint

- Scientific Linux
- Raspbian
- Android

How are these distros related to one another?

*Task 2:*

If you haven't already done so, consider that you are about to install a Linux distro for the first time. Think about what your needs would be on a desktop, or a server, or both. Then take this quiz: https://distrochooser.de/en

*Task 3:*

Make a note of your results from Task 2. Visit the websites of any distros that look interesting to you. What are their use cases and development philosophies (if any)?

*Task 4:*

Now it is time to install a Linux distro for use in the rest of the labs. For simplicity, we will assume the use of **Ubuntu 18.04 LTS**. However, if you are an advanced user, you are encouraged to try these labs on another distro of your choice.

Here is a great guide on how to install Ubuntu 18.04 in VirtualBox:

> https://linuxhint.com/install_ubuntu_18-04_virtualbox/

**Notes:**

Many distributions have a "Live USB" that you can test out without having to erase a computer's hard drive. You can also use VirtualBox, or another hypervisor, to test any number of Linux distros. Nearly every distro should run in a VM without trouble.

In subsequent labs, we will assume the use of an Ubuntu 18.04 LTS VM running on VirtualBox. This is by no means the only possibility, and once you've practiced the labs a few times, we encourage you to experiment with other distros!

> https://upload.wikimedia.org/wikipedia/commons/1/1b/Linux_Distribution_Timeline.svg

# LAB 2

# Major Open Source Applications: Desktop

**Lab Objective:**
Learn about common Linux desktop applications and how to install new applications using a package manager.

**Lab Purpose:**
Linux has a variety of open-source desktop software, serving the same functions as common proprietary software on other operating systems. In this lab, you will learn about some popular open-source software, and how to install and update said software using a tool called a package manager.

**Lab Tool:**
Ubuntu 18.04 (or another distro of your choice)

**Lab Topology:**
A single Linux machine, or virtual machine

**Lab Walkthrough:**

*Task 1:*
A default Ubuntu desktop has some common software already installed. See if you can locate, and familiarize yourself with, the following applications:

- LibreOffice—Office suite
- Thunderbird—Mail client
- Firefox—Web browser

Can't find these? Click "Show Applications" in the lower lefthand corner, then you can search for an application in the search box:

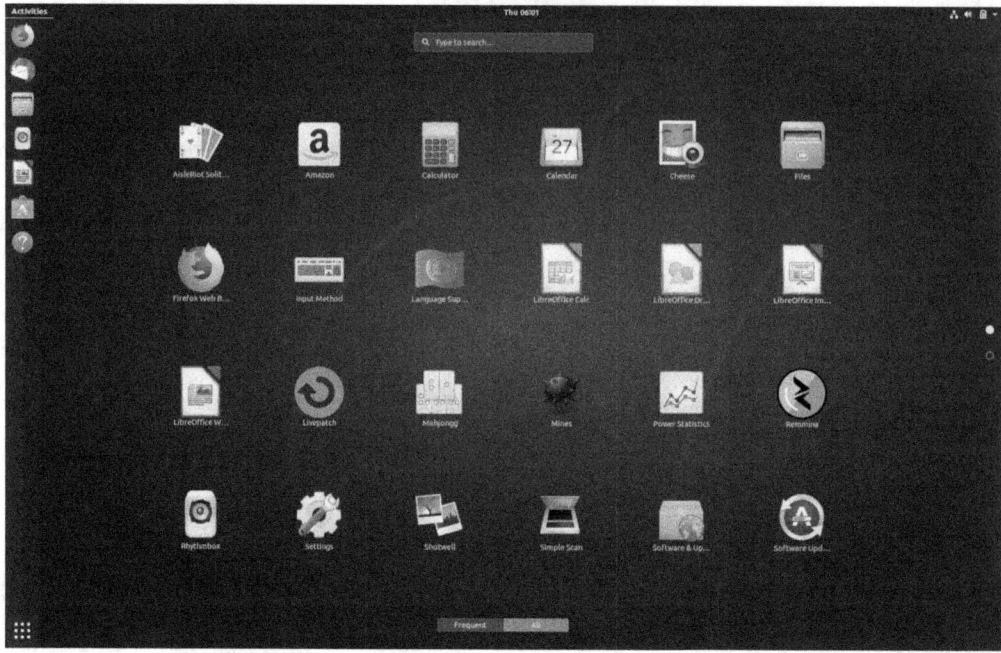

## Task 2:

As just one example, you will now configure Thunderbird to connect to an e-mail account. Upon opening Thunderbird for the first time, you should be greeted with a dialog like this:

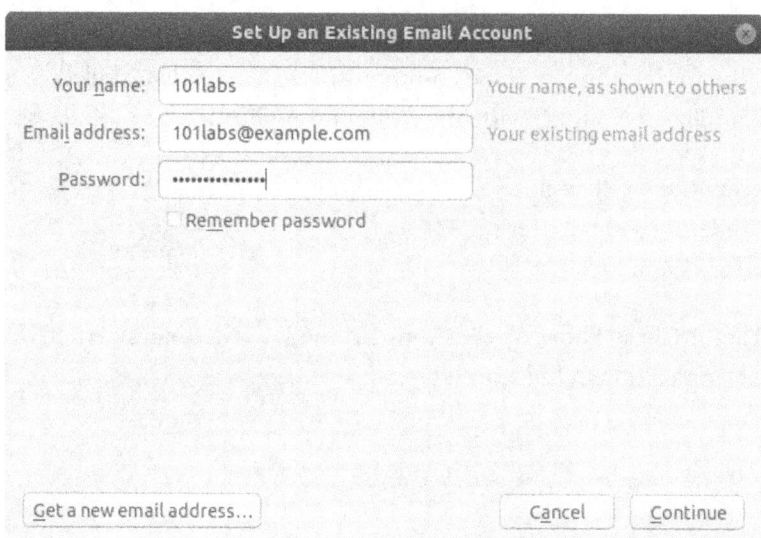

## LAB 2–MAJOR OPEN SOURCE APPLICATIONS: DESKTOP

Enter the details for your e-mail account, then click Continue. Many common mail providers are included in Mozilla's own database and will require no further configuration. For example, if you have a Gmail account, Thunderbird will set it up for you automatically once you've provided credentials.

If your e-mail service is not auto-configured, you will have to click "Manual config" (on the next screen) to enter your server details. Check with your mail provider for the correct values to enter.

*Task 3:*
What if you want to use an application that isn't already installed? You will have to install it! Fortunately, with Linux package managers, this is easy to do. Search for "GIMP" and install it with Ubuntu Software. Then, familiarize yourself with GIMP as well. GIMP is an image editing application.

*Task 4:*
Under the hood, Ubuntu Software uses a package manager called *apt*. Different Linux distros use different package managers, but their primary purpose is the same—to provide a centralized location from which to install and update thousands of common software packages.

Can you match the following distros below with their default package managers?

| | | |
|---|---|---|
| Arch | | yum |
| CentOS | dnf | |
| Debian | | pacman |
| Fedora | | Zypper |
| Gentoo | apt | |
| SUSE | | Portage |

**Notes:**
Sometimes, you may need to install a package that is not available in a distro's package management repositories (repos). In this case, you will either need to add additional repos, or install the package manually with a tool like *dpkg*.

# LAB 3

## Major Open Source Applications: Server

**Lab Objective:**
Learn about some software and development tools commonly deployed on Linux servers.

**Lab Purpose:**
In this lab, you will survey several common Linux server software tools. Though configuring these tools in detail is outside the scope of this lab, it is important to familiarize yourself with their applications.

**Lab Tool:**
Ubuntu 18.04 (or another distro of your choice)

**Lab Topology:**
A single Linux machine, or virtual machine

**Lab Walkthrough:**

*Task 1:*
Use a web browser on your Linux VM to research some of the following common Linux server applications:

- Web Servers: Apache httpd, nginx
- Databases: MariaDB, MySQL
- File Servers: NFS, Samba
- Private "Clouds": Nextcloud, ownCloud

In what situations would you deploy each application?

*Task 2:*
Are you familiar with any programming languages, such as…

- C?
- Java?

- JavaScript?
- Perl?
- Python?
- PHP?
- Something else?

If you have any software development experience, you might like to search in Ubuntu Software or another package manager for your favorite language tools. All of these languages and many more are supported on Linux.

*Task 3:*

Now, you will connect to a remote Linux server. First, use Ubuntu Software to install an application called PuTTY. PuTTY is a graphical version of an SSH/Telnet client, commonly used to connect to remote Linux servers, especially from Windows machines.

Upon running PuTTY, you will be greeted with a connection screen. Type in "towel.blinkenlights.nl", select Telnet, then click Open:

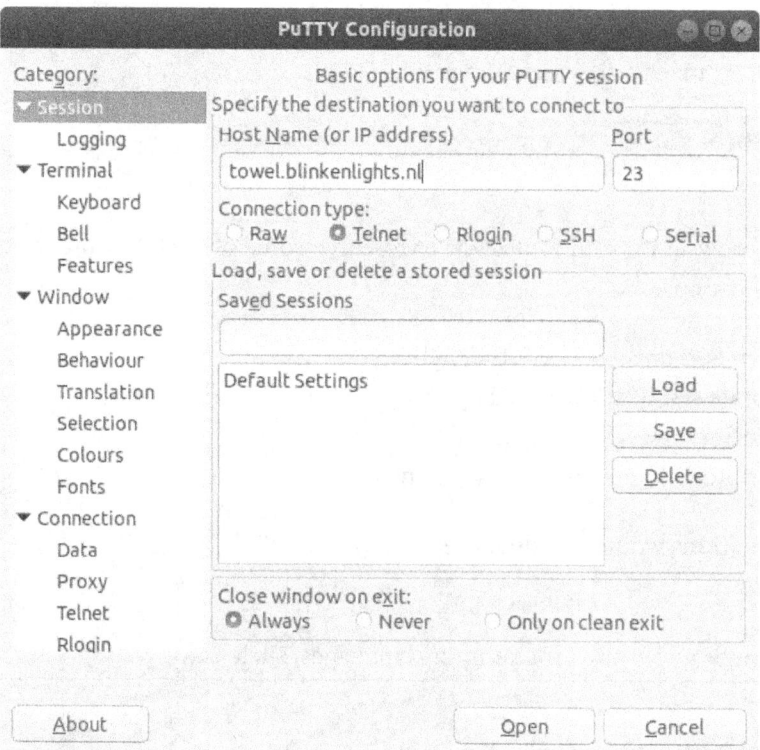

## Lab 3–Major Open Source Applications: Server

Now, enjoy the show!

It goes without saying that this particular Linux server is atypical—however, you will use a very similar process, either in PuTTY or on the command line, to connect to any remote Linux server.

*Task 4:*

Finally, locate the Terminal application. When you launch Terminal, it runs a special application called a shell. The default and most common shell is called Bash, but there are other options.

In practice, you will most often use the Terminal directly rather than a GUI application like PuTTY.

**Notes:**

Though less important on a modern desktop machine, the shell is a critical feature for managing Linux servers. In future labs, we will dive into the shell.

# LAB 4

# Open Source Software and Licensing

**Lab Objective:**
Learn about open source philosophy and different forms of open source software licensing.

**Lab Purpose:**
When working with open source software, particularly in business, it is important to recognize the implications of various licenses and business models.

**Lab Tool:**
A device with a web browser

**Lab Topology:**
N/A

**Lab Walkthrough:**

*Task 1:*
Explore choosealicense.com and try to answer the following questions:

- What is the difference between a copyleft license and a permissive license?
- What are the differences between GPL, BSD, and Creative Commons?
- Which licenses are compatible with each other when packaging software (and which ones aren't)?

*Task 2:*
Next, consider or read about some potential open-source business models. Can you identify how each business/service below monetizes open source software?

- Apple
- Canonical
- Mozilla
- MySQL (Oracle)

- RedHat
- Wikipedia
- WordPress

**Notes:**

Keep in mind that some potential business models are considered unethical by many members of the open-source community.

# LAB 5

# ICT Skills and Working in Linux

**Lab Objective:**
Make your Linux VM "your own" by doing some basic configuration and learning how to use common tools.

**Lab Purpose:**
The goal of this lab is to learn how to do some simple customizations of common Linux tools.

**Lab Tool:**
Ubuntu 18.04 (or another distro of your choice)

**Lab Topology:**
A single Linux machine, or virtual machine

**Lab Walkthrough:**

*Task 1:*
Open the Firefox web browser and explore its configuration. Click the menu in the upper-righthand corner, then click Preferences.

Consider tweaking some of Firefox's privacy and security settings. For example:

- Are all trackers and third-party cookies blocked by default?
- What is the default search engine? Is that acceptable to you?
- What kind of data does Firefox collect on you? Would you like to change that?
- What are the history and password-saving settings?

*Task 2:*
Now, you might like to install an add-on to Firefox. Use the search engine you chose to look for an add-on that might enhance Firefox in some way. Ad blocking, tab management, development tools, there are plenty of options!

*Task 3:*

If you haven't already, add the Terminal application in Ubuntu to your Favorites. You'll be using it a lot!

1. Click "Show Applications" in the bottom left corner, and search for Terminal.
2. Right-click the Terminal application and click "Add to Favorites".

*Task 4:*

Now we're going to change your Ubuntu password, via the command line. Open the Terminal application, then enter: `passwd`

You will first need to type your current password, then type your new password twice. None of these passwords will show anything being typed at all, which can be a bit jarring at first! However, in the end, you should see the message: `passwd: password updated successfully`

**Notes:**

So far in these labs, you have primarily used the desktop form of Linux. However, in industry, Linux has a far larger share on servers. How do large tech companies and industry professionals typically use Linux, and virtualization, on a daily basis?

# LAB 6

# Command Line Basics: Syntax and Quoting

**Lab Objective:**
Learn basic Linux commands and shell syntax.

**Lab Purpose:**
The Bash command shell is pre-installed on millions of Linux computers around the world. Understanding how this shell works is a critical skill for working with Linux.

**Lab Tool:**
Ubuntu 18.04 (or another distro of your choice)

**Lab Topology:**
A single Linux machine, or virtual machine

**Lab Walkthrough:**

*Task 1:*
Open the Terminal application, then enter: `echo Hello World`

The `echo` command simply prints out all of the "words," or arguments, that you give to it. This might not seem very useful, until...

*Task 2:*
Now enter the following four commands, in order:

```
quote='cat /etc/issue'
backquote=`cat /etc/issue`
echo $quote
echo $backquote
```

Here, `quote` and `backquote` are called *variables*. In the first two lines, we set them to the values `'cat /etc/issue'` and `` `cat /etc/issue` ``, respectively. (We'll get to the difference between quotes and backquotes in a minute.) In the last two lines, we reference the variables by putting $ before them, and print out their contents.

*Task 3:*

To understand single quotes, double quotes, and backquotes, enter the following:

```
hello="echo hello"
echo "$hello"
echo '$hello'
echo `$hello`
```

The output should be as follows:

```
echo hello
$hello
hello
```

Double quotes allow for variables to have their values referenced. Single quotes are always literal, while backquotes *execute* the command (including variable references) within those quotes.

**Notes:**

In some cases, you will want to reference variables with the ${variable} syntax. This is equivalent to $variable, but the reasons for choosing one over the other are beyond the scope of this lab.

Backquotes also have an alternative syntax:

```
$(echo hello)
```

This syntax is generally preferred over backquotes. We only mention backquotes to distinguish them from single quotes and ensure the differences are clear.

# LAB 7

# Command Line Basics: Environment Variables, Types, and History

**Lab Objective:**
Learn about Bash environment variables, types, and how to use the shell history.

**Lab Purpose:**
The Bash command shell is pre-installed on millions of Linux computers around the world. Understanding how this shell works is a critical skill for working with Linux.

**Lab Tool:**
Ubuntu 18.04 (or another distro of your choice)

**Lab Topology:**
A single Linux machine, or virtual machine

**Lab Walkthrough:**

*Task 1:*
Open the Terminal application, then enter: `echo $PATH`

The PATH environment variable lists all locations that Bash will search when you enter a command with a *relative* path. A *relative* path example is `bash`, compared to `/bin/bash`, which is an *absolute* path.

There are other environment variables as well. You can view all of them, and their values, using the `env` command.

*Task 2:*
You can add or modify an environment variable with `export`. For example:

    export PATH=${PATH}:./

In most cases, this change will disappear when you exit Bash, but the advantage of `export` is that child processes will now be able to see the new/modified variable.

## Task 3:

Another useful Bash command is called `type`. Use `type` to figure out information on other commands or functions:

```
type -a date
type -a if
type -a echo
type -a ls
```

## Task 4:

Enter `history` to see a history of commands you have typed into Bash.

To repeat a command, simply enter ! and then the appropriate number. For example. !12 will execute command #12 in the history list.

If you accidentally saved a password or other sensitive information to the history, you may use, for example, `history -d 47` to delete command #47 from the list, or even `history -c` to clear the history altogether.

If you want to save your current shell's history to another file, use `history -w filename`

**Notes:**

If you wish to permanently modify an environment variable or other shell settings, look into the `.bashrc` and `.bash_profile` files.

# LAB 8

# Using the Command Line to Get Help

**Lab Objective:**
Learn how to read various manuals from the command line.

**Lab Purpose:**
In a world of Google, Stack Overflow, and Wikipedia, sometimes we forget that Linux comes with its own library of documentation!

**Lab Tool:**
Ubuntu 18.04 (or another distro of your choice)

**Lab Topology:**
A single Linux machine, or virtual machine

**Lab Walkthrough:**

*Task 1:*
In Linux, there are three fairly reliable ways to obtain information on a given tool. Not every tool has all three options available. The `date` command does, so we will use it as an example.

Open the Terminal application, then enter: `date --help`

This is the quick, concise way of finding information about a given command. Most commands support either the `--help` or `-h` flags. Sometimes, though, you will run into a command that doesn't, or you just need more information than the quick help offers...

*Task 2:*
Enter: `man date`

`man` is short for manual, and is the most common way to provide documentation. Unlike quick help flags, it also is not limited to commands—you can use `man` pages to get information about system and library calls, special files, file formats, and even `man` itself (try entering `man man`).

***Task 3:***
Enter: `info date`

When even `man` isn't enough, sometimes you may need to rely on `info`. `info` is not the most convenient tool for casual browsing, but it provides the most details on any given aspect of a Linux system.

**Notes:**
Using unknown flags, like `--help` and `-h`, could potentially be risky, especially when a command is run as root. Do you understand why?

# LAB 9

## Using Directories and Listing Files: Files

**Lab Objective:**
Learn how to create, delete, and list files.

**Lab Purpose:**
In this lab, you will learn how to create, delete, and list files using the Bash shell.

**Lab Tool:**
Ubuntu 18.04 (or another distro of your choice)

**Lab Topology:**
A single Linux machine, or virtual machine

**Lab Walkthrough:**

*Task 1:*
Open the Terminal application, then enter: `touch foo`

You have now created a file, whose (empty) contents you can print with `cat foo`

You can list more details about the new file with `ls -lh foo`

*Task 2:*
Now create another empty file: `touch .bar`

You can use the `ls` command by itself to list all files in the current *directory* (which right now should be your *home directory*). But what happens when you do this now? Where is .bar?

.bar is a *hidden file*! Use `ls -a` and it will show up.

*Task 3:*
Now let's clean up. Enter `rm foo .bar` to remove both files you created.

**Notes:**

When you typed `ls -a`, you probably noticed some other strange dotted entries, like . and ..—these are not files, but directories, and will be covered in the next lab.

# LAB 10

## Using Directories and Listing Files: Directories

**Lab Objective:**
Learn how to create, delete, enumerate, and navigate directories.

**Lab Purpose:**
In this lab, you will learn how to create, delete, enumerate, and navigate amongst directories using the Bash shell.

**Lab Tool:**
Ubuntu 18.04 (or another distro of your choice)

**Lab Topology:**
A single Linux machine, or virtual machine

**Lab Walkthrough:**

*Task 1:*
Open the Terminal application, then enter: `mkdir -p foo/bar`

You have now created not one, but two directories, one inside the other. Now run the following:

```
cd foo
ls
```

Just like with files, you can also create hidden directories:

```
mkdir .baz
ls
ls -alh
```

Your *current directory* (which you changed with `cd`) is foo, which you can confirm with `pwd`.

*Task 2:*

`ls -alh` lists bar and .baz, as expected, but it also lists . and ..—these represent the *listed* and *parent* directories, respectively. In other words, . is foo, and .. is your home directory, also known as ~

Now run:

```
cd .
pwd
pushd ..
pwd
popd
pwd
cd ~
pwd
```

How do those commands affect your navigation through the directory structure?

*Task 3:*

Now run:

```
cd ./foo
touch ~/foo/.baz/quux
ls -aR ~/foo
```

The ~ expands to /home/user (where "user" is whatever your username is). Thus, while the first command above uses a *relative* pathname, where the result depends on the current directory, the latter two commands use an *absolute* pathname. The results of those commands will be the same regardless of your directory location (unless, of course, you switch users).

*Task 4:*

Finally, let's clean up:

```
cd ~
rm -r foo
```

**Notes:**

A "trick" you may run into is a file that begins with -, tricking Bash into thinking you are providing a flag to `rm` rather than the file to be removed. Can you figure out how to remove such a file?

# LAB 11

## Creating, Moving, and Deleting Files

**Lab Objective:**
Learn how to copy, move, and manage larger numbers of files.

**Lab Purpose:**
In this lab, you will learn the difference between copying and moving a file, and how simple shell globbing works.

**Lab Tool:**
Ubuntu 18.04 (or another distro of your choice)

**Lab Topology:**
A single Linux machine, or virtual machine

**Lab Walkthrough:**

*Task 1:*
Open the Terminal application, then enter:

```
mkdir lab11
cd lab11
touch f1 f2 f3
```

You now have a single directory containing three empty files.

*Task 2:*

```
cp f1 f4
ls
```

As expected, the `cp` command has created a fourth empty file. However, what happens when you do the following?

```
cp f1 f3
```

The f3 file gets overwritten—hope you didn't have any important data in there!

To prevent this, use either the `-i` or `-n` flag. `-i` stands for *interactive*, which means you will be prompted before overwriting. `-n` stands for *no-clobber*, which means the target file will never be overwritten. However, cp won't warn you about this, so `-i` is recommended for general shell usage.

*Task 3:*
Now run:

```
mv f1 f5
```

mv is the move command, so this does what you might expect, effectively renaming f1 to f5. Like cp, mv also has `-i` and `-n` flags, which have the same effects.

*Task 4:*
Now run:

```
mkdir foo bar
mv f2 foo
mv f3 foo
mv f* bar
```

What do you predict the final directory structure will look like? Now check it with `ls -aR bar`—did it match your prediction? (See **Answer 1** below.)

What you did with `f*` is called *globbing*. That command matched every file *and* directory starting with f (but not F—like everything else in Linux, globbing is case-sensitive), so f4, f5, and foo were all moved into bar.

*Task 5:*
Copy foo back to the current directory, with `cp bar/foo ./`

… Whoops! What happened? In order to copy a directory with its contents, you must use the `-r` flag (for *recursive*): `cp -r bar/foo ./`

*Task 6:*
Finally, let's clean up:

```
cd ~
rm -r lab11
```

## Lab 11–Creating, Moving, and Deleting Files

**Answer 1:**

```
bar:
.   ..      f4      f5      foo
bar/foo:
.   ..      f2      f3
```

**Notes:**

Be careful with `rm -r`—that command removes an entire directory without prompting you. Many horror stories can be found on the internet of people inadvertently deleting important files when they weren't paying attention!

# LAB 12

## Archiving Files on the Command Line

**Lab Objective:**
Learn how to create, extract, and examine various types of archive files.

**Lab Purpose:**
In this lab, you will learn about zip, gzip, bzip2, and xz compressed archives—as well as a tool, called `tar`, to manage most Linux archive types.

**Lab Tool:**
Ubuntu 18.04 (or another distro of your choice)

**Lab Topology:**
A single Linux machine, or virtual machine

**Lab Walkthrough:**

*Task 1:*
Open the Terminal application and run the following:

```
mkdir lab12
cd lab12
touch f1 f2 f3 f4 f5 f6 f7 f8 f9
```

*Task 2:*
If you've worked with Windows, you may be familiar with ZIP files. ZIP is a common type of archive which both compresses and stores files.

Run:

```
zip files.zip f*
unzip -l files.zip
```

You can see that all nine files are included in files.zip, although since they were empty there was nothing to compress. You can unzip this archive with `unzip files.zip`, but you will be prompted to overwrite the existing files.

Finally, clean up with `rm files.zip`

*Task 3:*
Though ZIP is a common format and well-supported on Linux, it is not the main compression format Linux uses. That would be the classic gzip:

```
gzip f*
ls
```

Wait a minute... why are there now nine gzipped files instead of just one? And what happened to the originals?

This is why gzip is considered a *compression* format rather than an *archive* one. To create a single, easy-to-use archive file, we need a different tool...

*Task 4:*
Run: `tar -cf files.tar.gz f*`

Now, with the help of the *tar archiver*, you have your gzipped archive in files.tar.gz... well, sort of.

Normally, with a gzipped tarball, you would be able to extract it with `tar -xf files.tar.gz` and get all of the original files back. Instead, you could try that yourself now, and you would get the nine .gz files.

There's a better way. Let's blow this up and start over:

```
rm f*
touch f1 f2 f3 f4 f5 f6 f7 f8 f9
tar -czf archive.tar.gz f*
tar --list -f archive.tar.gz
```

Ta-da! Now you see a list of nine files within your single compressed tarball.

*Task 5:*
gzip isn't the only format you can use with `tar`:

```
tar -cjf archive.tar.bz2 f*
tar -cJf archive.tar.xz f*
```

The bzip2 and XZ formats, respectively, are newer and use different algorithms from gzip, but the end result is the same. `tar` can extract all of its formats in the same way, simply by using `tar -xf filename`.

*Task 6:*

Finally, clean up:

```
cd ~
rm -r lab12
```

**Notes:**

ZIP, gzip, bzip2, and XZ all have their own strengths and weaknesses. You could look for benchmarks on the internet... or, for an extra challenge, you could try running your own! You should have ZIP installed but you might have to do so if for some reason it's not present.

# LAB 13

# Searching and Extracting Data from Files: Pipes and Redirection

**Lab Objective:**
Learn how to use pipes and redirect input and output in Bash.

**Lab Purpose:**
Bash has two commonly-used features, known as pipes and I/O redirection, that make life easier when using Linux. In this lab, you will learn how to make use of these powerful features.

**Lab Tool:**
Ubuntu 18.04 (or another distro of your choice)

**Lab Topology:**
A single Linux machine, or virtual machine

**Lab Walkthrough:**

*Task 1:*
Open the Terminal application and run:

```
mkdir lab13
cd lab13
echo "hello world" > hello
cat hello
```

You just *redirected* the output from your `echo` command into the hello file. The > is a shortcut; the proper version of this would be 1>, where 1 is called a *file descriptor*, which references the *standard output*.

*Task 2:*
Now run:

```
ls nonexistent 2>> hello
cat hello
```

Based on the new contents of the hello file ("ls: cannot access 'nonexistent': No such file or directory"), what can you surmise about the function of 2>>? Here, 2 is a file descriptor for *standard error*.

*Task 3:*
Sometimes, you want to redirect both output *and* error to the same place. In ye olden days, you would have to do something ugly like this: `ls foo > bar 2>&1`

However, modern versions of Bash have an easy-to-use shortcut: `ls foo &> bar`

*Task 4:*
We've talked about redirecting output, but what about input? To learn about that, run the following commands:

```
cat < hello

read foo <<< "foo"
echo $foo

cat << END-OF-FILE > goodbye
hello
goodbye
END-OF-FILE
cat goodbye
```

In short: < redirects input from a file name, << starts a here document, and <<< redirects input from another command.

*Task 5:*
Pipes (|) let you use the output of a command as the input to another command. In many situations (but not all), | and <<< are kind of a reverse of one another. For example, the output of...

```
echo "hello world" | grep e
```

... is identical to the output of...

```
grep e <<< "hello world"
```

Try to predict the output of the following command string before you run it (see **Answer 1** below):

```
grep non hello | cut -d: -f3
```

## Lab 13–Searching and Extracting Data from Files: Pipes and Redirection

*Task 6:*

Finally, clean up:

```
cd ~
rm -r lab13
```

**Answer 1:**

```
No such file or directory
```

**Notes:**

`grep` searches for matching patterns in a string, while `cut` splits the input into pieces. Both are very common tools which you will use more in subsequent labs.

# LAB 14

# Searching and Extracting Data from Files: Regular Expressions

**Lab Objective:**
Learn how to use regular expressions for complex string pattern matching.

**Lab Purpose:**
Regular expressions are a tool used commonly in Linux to match complex patterns in strings and text files. Many tools support regular expressions.

**Lab Tool:**
Ubuntu 18.04 (or another distro of your choice)

**Lab Topology:**
A single Linux machine, or virtual machine

**Lab Walkthrough:**

*Task 1:*
Open the Terminal application. See if you can predict what the output of this command sequence will be before you run it (see **Answer 1** below):

```
echo "foo
bar
baz
quux
frob
plugh
xyzzy" | sort | tail -5 | grep [be]
```

## Task 2:

Can you match which of the following strings (on the right) would match each regular expression (on the left)? Each regex may have multiple matches! See **Answer 2** below for the solution.

| | |
|---|---|
| ^s?.*$ | Hello World |
| ^[0-9]  .*$ | 1, 2, 3, Go! |
| ^.*[a-z].*$ | sayonara |
| ^q?[a-z]*$ | 101labs |

**Answer 1:**

```
frob
```

**Answer 2:**

> The first expression matches all four strings.
> The second expression matches "1, 2, 3, Go!" and "101labs".
> The third expression matches all four strings.
> The fourth expression matches "sayonara".

**Notes:**

Regexr is a great resource for practicing your regular expressions.

# LAB 15

## Turning Commands into a Script: Shell Scripting

**Lab Objective:**
Learn how to write a simple shell script containing multiple commands.

**Lab Purpose:**
Scripting with Bash is a daily task by many professional Linux administrators. When a task is repetitive, you don't want to be typing the same list of commands over and over; you want to create a script, and perhaps also schedule that script to run automatically.

**Lab Tool:**
Ubuntu 18.04 (or another distro of your choice)

**Lab Topology:**
A single Linux machine, or virtual machine

**Lab Walkthrough:**

*Task 1:*
Open the Terminal application, and run your favorite text editor, such as `vi` or `nano`. (If you have never used `vi` or `vim`, then `nano` is strongly recommended.)

Create a file with the following contents:

```
#!/bin/bash
for (( n=0; n<$1; n++ ))
do
   echo $n
done
echo "Output from $0 complete."
```

*Task 2:*
Make the file executable (with `chmod +x filename`), then run it like:

```
./filename 10
```

You should see the numbers 0-9 printed out, one at a time. Knowing what the script does now, can you understand it in its entirety? What happens if you fail to pass an argument, or if you pass "gibberish," like letters instead of a number?

*Task 3:*
Run your script without an argument. Then run: `echo $?`

`$?` is a special variable that references the *exit status*. In a successful program, the exit status would be 0. Please try it for yourself now. Then edit the script by removing the last echo statement. This script then fails without an argument, returning a different exit status.

**Notes:**
That first line, starting with `#!` (called a *shebang*), denotes what program will be used to interpret your script. Usually, this is `/bin/bash`, but it can also be another shell like `/bin/zsh`, or even another programming language like `/usr/bin/python`.

In this case, you could remove the shebang line, because your interpreter is the same (Bash) as the shell you are currently running. But you should always include it because you never know when you might want to share a script with someone using a different shell.

# LAB 16

## Turning Commands into a Script: Scripting Practice

**Lab Objective:**
Use what you already know to write a simple shell script, from scratch.

**Lab Purpose:**
Scripting with Bash is a daily task by many professional Linux administrators. When a task is repetitive, you don't want to be typing the same list of commands over and over; you want to create a script, and perhaps also schedule that script to run automatically.

**Lab Tool:**
Ubuntu 18.04 (or another distro of your choice)

**Lab Topology:**
A single Linux machine, or virtual machine

**Lab Walkthrough:**

*Task 1:*
Open the Terminal application, and run your favorite text editor, such as `vi` or `nano`. (If you have never used `vi` or `vim`, then `nano` is strongly recommended.)

You may wish to reference Lab 15 if you have not already done so. Your goal is to write a script which accepts one argument—a number—and prints out two numbers at a time such that:

- The first number counts down from the argument to 0
- The second number counts up from 0 to the argument

Example:

```
./foo.sh 100
100 0
99 1
98 2
...
```

If the user doesn't pass an argument, or passes an argument that doesn't make sense, like a word, you should print a friendly message like "Please give a number."

Remember to make the file executable (with `chmod +x filename`) before testing it. See **Answer 1** below for one possible solution.

**Answer 1:**

```
#!/bin/bash
if ! [ "$1" -ge 0 ]
then
    echo "Please give a number."
    exit 1
fi
for (( n=0; n<=$1; n++ ))
do
    echo $(($1-$n)) $n
done
```

**Notes:**

In Lab 15, you read about the exit status. For error-checking purposes: Can you figure out how to use the exit status before your script has exited?

# LAB 17

## Choosing an Operating System

**Lab Objective:**
Learn how to choose an operating system for your given purposes.

**Lab Purpose:**
Windows, OS X, and Linux each have their own strengths, weaknesses, and use cases. In this lab you, will review those.

**Lab Tool:**
An internet-connected device with a web browser

**Lab Topology:**
N/A

**Lab Walkthrough:**

*Task 1:*
Unlike Windows and OS X, Linux offers nearly limitless variety in terms of versions or flavors, called "distros." Linux is created by a community of developers and runs on nearly any hardware in existence. Linux distributions were discussed in Lab 1. Explore Distrochooser and Distrowatch to learn more about the many Linux distros.

*Task 2:*
OS X is a proprietary operating system created by Apple, and designed to run only on Apple hardware. Modern OS X has Unix at its core, but comes with a heavily redesigned Apple user interface, among other modifications. OS X combines a functional graphical user interface with a number of familiar tools for Unix administrators.

*Task 3:*
Windows is a proprietary operating system created by Microsoft. Though proprietary, it still runs on a wide variety of hardware (though not as wide a variety as Linux). In terms of administration, Windows has traditionally focused less on command-line tools and

more on graphical tools. However, in recent years, this has begun to change with the advent of PowerShell, at least on server versions of Windows.

**Notes:**

Even though the LPIC exams focus on Linux, spend any time as a Linux professional and it is inevitable that you will at some point be asked to provide interoperability with other operating systems. Learning the basics of Windows and OS X, as well as Linux tools meant to interoperate with them (such as Samba), will assist you in this.

# LAB 18

# Understanding Computer Hardware

**Lab Objective:**
Learn what hardware goes into building a computer and how to interface with some hardware from Linux.

**Lab Purpose:**
The following are primary hardware components in desktop and server computers:

- Motherboard
- Processor(s)
- Memory
- Power suppl(y/ies)
- Hard/solid-state disks
- Optical drives
- Peripherals

**Lab Tool:**
Ubuntu 18.04 (or another distro of your choice)

**Lab Topology:**
A single Linux machine, or virtual machine

**Lab Walkthrough:**

*Task 1:*
Open the Terminal and run the following commands to review some of the hardware (real or virtualized) which is powering your Linux computer:

- `lscpu`
- `lspci`
- `lsusb -t`
- `sudo lshw`
- `sudo hdparm -i /dev/sd*`

## Task 2:

Now investigate some related low-level resources, like partitions, drivers (kernel modules), and resource usage:

- `sudo fdisk -l`
- `lsmod`
- `df -h`
- `free -m`

**Notes:**

If you want hardware information that you don't know how to find, a good way to start is by exploring the /proc filesystem. Most of the tools listed above simply gather and format information from /proc; that is where the kernel presents it.

# LAB 19

# Where Data is Stored: Processes and Configuration

**Lab Objective:**
Learn how to manage running processes and program configurations.

**Lab Purpose:**
In this lab, you will learn how to configure various system processes and how to manage and monitor those processes while they are running.

**Lab Tool:**
Ubuntu 18.04 (or another distro of your choice)

**Lab Topology:**
A single Linux machine, or virtual machine

**Lab Walkthrough:**

*Task 1:*
Open the Terminal and run `ls /boot`

The contents will vary, but generally what you will see is a Linux kernel file (name starting with `vmlinuz`), initrd file, System.map, a `grub` configuration directory, and sometimes a copy of the kernel configuration.

Everything in this directory, including the `grub` config file (`/boot/grub/grub.cfg`), is related—as you might expect—to your system boot processes. This is one directory you don't want to mess with unless you know what you're doing!

*Task 2:*
Next, run: `ls /etc`

In Linux parlance, 'etc' stands for 'editable text configuration.' `/etc` is the primary directory tree for all system configuration; with few exceptions, nearly all configurations are stored in, or linked from, `/etc`.

The few (non-user-specific) exceptions might be in /dev, /sys or /proc. These are special, dynamically-generated filesystems. You may occasionally read information from these filesystems, but most of the time you shouldn't be writing directly to them.

## Task 3:
Run the following commands in your Terminal:

- `free -m`
- `ps -ef`
- `top`        # press q to quit

These are three common tools to monitor processes and their resource usage. (Got a runaway process that won't quit via the normal means? Try `kill` or `pkill`.)

**Notes:**
/dev contains special files called device nodes, which are linked to device drivers. /sys and /proc contain files by which the kernel presents non-process and process-related information, respectively. (In reality, this is more muddled, but that is the ideal separation.)

# LAB 20

# Where Data is Stored: System Messaging and Logging

**Lab Objective:**
Learn how to view system messages and logs.

**Lab Purpose:**
In this lab, you will learn how to debug your system (or just get a glimpse at what's going on) by viewing log messages.

**Lab Tool:**
Ubuntu 18.04 (or another distro of your choice)

**Lab Topology:**
A single Linux machine, or virtual machine

**Lab Walkthrough:**

*Task 1:*
Open your Terminal and run `dmesg`

The `man` (manual) page for `dmesg` states that it is used to "examine or control the kernel ring buffer." To put it simply, you can use `dmesg` to view boot logs and other logs your distro considers important.

*Task 2:*
Run `ls -aR /var/log`

This is the main storage directory for all system logs (although, see the Notes). If you peruse some of the log files, you may find some of the same logs that were printed by `dmesg`. In particular, look at the `/var/log/syslog` file.

Configuration of `rsyslog` is outside the scope of this lab, but through `rsyslog` you can record logs of all severities, write them to different files, e-mail them, or even print emergency alert messages to the console for all users to see.

*Task 3:*

You can use `tail` to monitor logs in real-time. Run: `sudo tail -f /var/log/auth.log`

Then, in a separate Terminal window or tab, run `sudo -i` three times. When prompted for your password, do each of the following once:

- Type Ctrl+C to cancel the command.
- Intentionally mistype your password.
- Type your password correctly.

Check the tab where `tail` is running to see what is logged as a result of your actions. This is a simple, but accurate, method of keeping tabs on `sudo` users on a system.

**Notes:**

In recent years, traditional logging tools have been supplanted in some distros by `systemd`, which uses `journalctl` to manage logs. In practice, you should familiarize yourself with both log management techniques.

# LAB 21

## Your Computer on the Network

**Lab Objective:**
Learn how to manage networking on Linux computers.

**Lab Purpose:**
In this lab, you will learn how to query important network configuration and gather information for connecting a Linux computer to a Local Area Network.

**Lab Tool:**
Ubuntu 18.04 (or another distro of your choice)

**Lab Topology:**
A single Linux machine, or virtual machine

**Lab Walkthrough:**

*Task 1:*
Open your Terminal and run the following commands to gather information on your current network configuration:

- `ip addr show`
- `ip route show`
- `ss -ap`
- `cat /etc/hosts`
- `cat /etc/resolv.conf`

Does your local network support IPv4, IPv6, or both?

*Task 2:*
Now turn off your Wi-Fi, or disconnect your Ethernet cable, or disable the network connection to your VM. Then run the first three of those commands again.

What changes occurred, and why?

*Task 3:*

Reconnect your network and gather some information on 101labs:

```
host -v 101labs.net
```

Can you `ping` 101labs.net? If not, how might you diagnose the problem?

*Task 4:*

Run `ip route show | grep default` and copy the output. You'll use it later!

Now, make sure to stop anything important you might be doing... then run: `sudo ip route del default`

Congratulations, you've just broken your internet connection by deleting the default route. You may confirm this by attempting to browse the internet with Firefox. In a real-world scenario, you could diagnose this problem by running `ip route show` and noting the lack of a default route.

To fix your connection, run: `sudo ip route add <extra>`, where <extra> is the output you copied earlier.

**Notes:**

The `net-tools` package, containing `netstat`, `ifconfig` and `route`, among other tools, is considered deprecated. Nevertheless, you may run into systems which only have these tools, and so should have a passing familiarity with them.

# LAB 22

# Basic Security and Identifying User Types

**Lab Objective:**
Learn how to identify the differences between the root user, standard users, and system users.

**Lab Purpose:**
In this lab, you will learn about the different types of Linux users and a few tools to identify and audit them.

**Lab Tool:**
Ubuntu 18.04 (or another distro of your choice)

**Lab Topology:**
A single Linux machine, or virtual machine

**Lab Walkthrough:**

*Task 1:*
Open the Terminal and run: `cat /etc/passwd`

This file is an inventory of all users on your system. The passwd file is a database with seven fields, separated by colons:

1. Username
2. Encrypted password (in practice, hardly ever used—see below)
3. User ID
4. Group ID
5. Comment
6. Home directory
7. Default shell

Take note of the *root* user, which should be listed on the first line. This is the administrative user, and is the only user that can unconditionally do anything on the system. By running a command preceded with `sudo`, you are running that command as the root user. (You can also use `sudo -i` or `su` to access a root shell directly.)

If you look at the user ID's, you will notice that most of them, on a default system, are below 1000. These are *system* users, typically used to run specific services, rather than running those as root, which can create security problems. On most systems, human user ID's begin at 1000 or 500.

You can easily see the passwd information for your own user with: `grep ^$USER /etc/passwd`

### Task 2:
Now run: `sudo cat /etc/shadow`

The shadow file is a sensitive database containing hashed user passwords, among other information. Be careful with the contents of this file! It contains nine fields, again, separated by colons—however, on a default Ubuntu install, only the first three are likely to be significant:

1. Username
2. Encrypted password
3. Date of last password change

The other fields contain information like account expiration dates and minimum/maximum password ages, which are not configured on a default system. See `man 5 shadow` for more information.

You can see this information for your own user with: `sudo grep ^$USER /etc/shadow`

### Task 3:
Now run: `cat /etc/group`

As you might expect, this is a database of all groups on the system. It contains four fields separated by colons:

1. Group name
2. Encrypted group password
3. Group ID
4. List of users who are members

## Lab 22–Basic Security and Identifying User Types

Run `groups` to learn which groups your user has membership in. You can get more information, including group ID's, with the `id` command.

*Task 4:*
Finally, a few commands you can use to audit user logins:

- `who`
- `w`
- `last`
- `last $USER      # For your own user`

**Notes:**
In the next lab, you will learn how to add regular users and system users. In practice, you will rarely need to add system users manually—these are typically added along with the services that use them.

# LAB 23

# Creating Users and Groups

**Lab Objective:**
Learn how to create and customize users and groups.

**Lab Purpose:**
In this lab, you will learn how to create users and groups, as well as set their passwords.

**Lab Tool:**
Ubuntu 18.04 (or another distro of your choice)

**Lab Topology:**
A single Linux machine, or virtual machine

**Lab Walkthrough:**

*Task 1:*
Open the Terminal and run:

```
sudo sh -c 'echo "Hello World" > /etc/skel/hello.txt'
```

Here, you are adding a file to the /etc/skel directory, which determines the default files in a new user's home directory.

Now:

- `sudo useradd -m foo`
- `sudo cat ~foo/hello.txt`

You should see the output "Hello World". What happened is that you created a new user, called foo (using the `-m` switch to ensure a home directory was created). Every file in /etc/skel was then copied to the new user's home directory.

Finally, set an initial password for this user with: `sudo passwd foo`

*Task 2:*
Now let's add a system user. Run: `sudo useradd -r bar`

When adding a system user, `useradd` does not add any account or password aging information, and sets a user ID appropriate for a system user (typically below 1000). It also does not create a home directory unless you specify `-m`.

*Task 3:*
Now let's create a group and add our new users to it:

- `sudo groupadd baz`
- `sudo usermod -a -G baz foo`
- `sudo usermod -a -G baz bar`

Verify that the users were added with: `grep ^baz /etc/group`

*Task 4:*
Finally, clean up:

- `sudo rm /etc/skel/hello.txt`
- `sudo userdel foo`
- `sudo userdel bar`
- `sudo groupdel baz`
- `sudo rm -r /home/foo`

**Notes:**
`usermod` is a very useful command for managing users. In addition to adding and removing users from groups, it allows you to manage account/password expirations and other security features.

# LAB 24

# Managing File Permissions and Ownership

**Lab Objective:**
Learn how to manipulate file permissions and ownership settings.

**Lab Purpose:**
In this lab, you will learn to use `chmod` and `chown`, as well as view permissions and ownership settings with `ls`.

**Lab Tool:**
Ubuntu 18.04 (or another distro of your choice)

**Lab Topology:**
A single Linux machine, or virtual machine

**Lab Walkthrough:**

*Task 1:*
Open the Terminal and run (you may need to add the user 'foo' if you removed it on the last lab):

- `echo "Hello World" > foo`
- `ls -l foo`

Look at the first field; you should see `-rw-r--r--`

This indicates the user, group, and other permissions. The last nine characters, in groups of three, denote these permissions. In this instance:

- `rw-` indicates read/write (but not execute) permissions for the user who owns the file
- `r--` indicates read-only permissions for the group that owns the file
- `r--` indicates read-only permissions for all non-owners, a.k.a. "world"

The first character indicates the type of file. In this case, it is a regular file; directories begin with `d`.

Who are the user and group owners of this file? The third and fourth fields of `ls -l` tell us that. By default, it should be your own user and primary group.

*Task 2:*
Now run:

- `sudo chown root foo`
- `ls -l foo`
- `cat foo`

You've just changed the user ownership to root, while keeping the group ownership. As the file has group- and world-read permissions, you can still see its contents.

*Task 3:*
Now run:

- `sudo chmod o-r foo`
- `ls -l foo`
- `cat foo`

That `chmod` command removes read permissions from other. However, as you still have group ownership, you can still see the file's contents.

*Task 4:*
Now run:

- `sudo chmod 600 foo`
- `ls -l foo`
- `cat foo`

This `chmod` command sets the permissions explicitly, to read-write for the owning user only. As that is root, we can no longer read the file.

*Task 5:*
Finally, clean up with `sudo rm foo`

**Notes:**
Execute permissions come into play on executable files as well as directories. If a user/group cannot "execute" a directory, it cannot view the contents of said directory or any subdirectories.

# LAB 25

## Special Directories and Files

**Lab Objective:**
Learn how to use temporary files and directories, symbolic links, and special permissions.

**Lab Purpose:**
In this lab, you will work with symbolic links, special file/directory permissions, and temporary files and directories.

**Lab Tool:**
Ubuntu 18.04 (or another distro of your choice)

**Lab Topology:**
A single Linux machine, or virtual machine

**Lab Walkthrough:**

*Task 1:*
Open the Terminal and run: `ls -ld /tmp`

Notice the permissions: `drwxrwxrwt`

The `t` at the end indicates what is called the *sticky bit*. This means that only users/groups who own a given file may modify it. This is important on world-writable directories, such as those holding temporary files, to prevent users from messing with other users' files.

*Task 2:*
Now run:

- `ln -sv $(mktemp) mytmp`
- `ls -l mytmp`
- `rm mytmp`

What just happened? `mktemp` created a randomly-named temporary file. Then you created a *symbolic link* to that file called mytmp. The `ls` output shows this link. A symbolic link is simply a reference to an existing file. This way, you may have multiple references to a single file—edit the original file, and all of the references instantly update. This is useful for some system configurations.

**Notes:**

In addition to /tmp, there is also /var/tmp, which is typically used for larger and/or longer-lasting temporary files. /tmp is usually cleaned on every reboot; the same is not necessarily true for /var/tmp.

# LPIC1 Linux Administrator–Exam 101

# LAB 26

# Determine and Configure Hardware Settings: PCI Devices and Peripherals

**Lab Objective:**
Learn about gathering information on and configuring PCI devices and peripherals.

**Lab Purpose:**
In this lab, you will use tools such as `lsusb` and `lspci` to determine hardware resources and manipulate USB and PCI devices.

**Lab Tool:**
Ubuntu 18.04 (or another distro of your choice)

**Lab Topology:**
A single Linux machine, or virtual machine

**Lab Walkthrough:**

*Task 1:*
Open the Terminal and run:

```
for dev in $(ls /sys/bus/usb/devices/*/product); do echo -n "$dev :";
cat $dev; done
```

The output will be a list of USB devices connected to your system, such as the following:

```
/sys/bus/usb/devices/1-1/product: USB Tablet
/sys/bus/usb/devices/usb1/product: OHCI PCI host controller
```

What we're interested in is the USB bus and port from the first field. In this example, there are two devices, a USB tablet at 1-1 and a PCI controller at usb1.

You may also use `lsusb` to gather more information on these devices.

## Task 2:

You will now **optionally** disable and re-enable one of the above USB devices. This is optional because if done incorrectly, it could render your system temporarily unusable until a reboot.

Let's say that you have a webcam at 1-1.6. This is safe to disable. You would run:

```
sudo sh -c 'echo 1.1-6 > /sys/bus/usb/drivers/usb/unbind'
```

Test the device you disabled to confirm that it is no longer available. To re-enable the device, simply run:

```
sudo sh -c 'echo 1.1-6 > /sys/bus/usb/drivers/usb/bind'
```

## Task 3:
Run: `lspci -v`

This is a list of your PCI devices. Take note of the devices which list kernel modules, on the last line beginning with "Kernel modules". You can confirm that these modules are loaded by getting a list of the currently loaded kernel modules with `lsmod`

Now you will remove, and reload, one of these modules. As in the previous step, you need to be careful which module you remove, as choosing the wrong one could render your system temporarily unusable.

Removing a sound module, such as snd_seq_midi, is safe. Run:

```
sudo modprobe -r snd_seq_midi
```

You may confirm that the module is removed with: `lsmod | grep snd_seq_midi`

Depending on the module you chose, this may or may not have any noticeable effect on functionality. There are many Linux kernel modules loaded on a typical system, though of course it best not to mess with them unless you know what they do!

Reload the module with: `sudo modprobe snd_seq_midi`

**Notes:**
It is good to understand the /proc and /sys filesystems—all information on USB and PCI devices is stored there, if you know where to look. The next lab will dive into these filesystems.

# LAB 27

# Determine and Configure Hardware Settings: Filesystems and Storage

**Lab Objective:**
Learn about gathering information on and configuring storage devices and special filesystems.

**Lab Purpose:**
In this lab, you will learn about how to differentiate between various types of mass storage devices, and about sysfs, udev, and dbus.

**Lab Tool:**
Ubuntu 18.04 (or another distro of your choice)

**Lab Topology:**
A single Linux machine, or virtual machine

**Lab Walkthrough:**

*Task 1:*
Open the Terminal and run `ls /sys/block`

This will give you a list of block devices on your system. At a minimum, you should have a device such as `sda` or `xvda`. These are your standard disk devices, like hard disks and USB drives. You may also have an optical drive, such as `sr0`, and possibly one or more loopback devices.

To get more information on these devices, run `lsblk`

This will list all of those devices as well as their sizes, types, and mount points. Your hard drive(s) should be labeled as "disk", partitions as "part", loopback devices as "loop", and optical or other read-only devices as "rom".

*Task 2:*
Choose a device from above; for example, /dev/sda.

Run: `udevadm info /dev/sda`

Udev is a Linux subsystem that deals with hardware events, like plugging and unplugging a USB keyboard. Here, we are using yet another tool to gather information on a hard disk device (or another device of your choice).

Notice the first line from the output, beginning with "P:". Tying back to sysfs, this is the path for said device under the /sys filesystem. You can confirm this with

`ls /sys/[path]`, where [path] is the output from the first line above.

Udev is also responsible for generating the device nodes in /dev on every boot. If you run `ls /dev`, you will see all of the devices you discovered earlier—plus many others.

*Task 3:*
D-Bus is a mechanism for inter-process communication (IPC). Run `dbus-monitor` and then open an application like Thunderbird. You will see a large number of messages being sent back and forth between various processes. You might need to use CTRL + C or q to quit.

**Notes:**
Challenge: Can you figure out how to suspend the system just by echoing a value to a file under sysfs?

# LAB 28

# Boot the System: Boot Sequence

**Lab Objective:**
Learn how to manage boot options and understand the boot sequence.

**Lab Purpose:**
In this lab, you will practice issuing commands to the boot loader, and gain a deeper understanding of the Linux boot process, from BIOS/UEFI to completion.

**Lab Tool:**
Ubuntu 18.04 (or another distro of your choice)

**Lab Topology:**
A single Linux machine, or virtual machine

**Lab Walkthrough:**

*Task 1:*
Open the Terminal and run:

- `sudo sed -i.bak -e 's/GRUB_TIMEOUT=0/GRUB_TIMEOUT=10/' -e 's/GRUB_TIMEOUT_STYLE=hidden/GRUB_TIMEOUT_STYLE=menu/' -e 's/GRUB_CMDLINE_LINUX_DEFAULT="quiet splash"/GRUB_CMDLINE_LINUX_DEFAULT=""/' /etc/default/grub`
- `sudo update-grub`

What you're doing here is modifying the GRUB bootloader so that you can see the boot menu and various logs.

Run `dmesg | grep ATA`—you are looking for a line indicating your hard disk, beginning with something like ata2.00 or ata3.00. Make a note of this number for later.

Finally, reboot your computer or VM.

*Task 2:*

Upon boot, you should be greeted with a GRUB menu. Hit 'c' to enter the GRUB prompt. Here, you can run various bootloader commands. Use `ls` to explore your partitions; the format looks a bit different, for example, (hd0,msdos1). There are also commands like `lsmod`, `lspci`, and `parttool`. Do these look familiar? Run `help` for a full list.

Then, hit ESC to return to the boot menu.

*Task 3:*

Back at the boot menu, hit 'e' to enter a screen where you can modify the boot commands. Depending on your implementation, there may be a lot here, but you are looking for a line beginning with "linux". This is the line that loads the Linux kernel, and is the most commonly modified line for editing boot options.

At the end of that line, append `libata.force=[number]:disable`, where `[number]` is the number you noted above, such as 3.00.

Now, hit Ctrl+X to boot your computer.

*Task 4:*

After a couple of minutes, you may notice that something has gone wrong! You have disabled your primary hard disk, causing Linux to be unable to boot. It may have *looked* like it was booting initially, though. That's because the next step of the boot process is to load the *initial RAM disk* (initrd), prior to loading the kernel. The initrd was successful whereas the kernel step failed, which is why you should have ended up at a `(initramfs)` prompt.

In short, the Linux boot process goes like this:

1. BIOS/UEFI enumerates hardware and loads code from the configured boot device (not Linux-specific).
2. GRUB bootloader loads, parses boot commands and options.
3. Initrd is loaded, bootstraps various filesystems and modules, and then loads the kernel.
4. The init process is launched, which in turn executes all startup processes as configured within Linux.

Type `reboot` to reboot your computer/VM and return it to normalcy.

## Lab 28–Boot the System: Boot Sequence

If you'd like to undo the GRUB changes made in step 1, just run:

- `sudo mv /etc/default/grub{.bak,}`
- `sudo update-grub`

**Notes:**

The reason an initial RAM disk is used is because Linux is a generic operating system meant to run on a wide variety of hardware and disk configurations. Having to enable checks for all of these configurations in the kernel directly would make the kernel much larger than necessary. Thus, a temporary filesystem is used to do all of the special case handling, and then load the correct modules along with the kernel.

# LAB 29

# Boot the System: SysVInit and Systemd

**Lab Objective:**
Learn how to manage SysVInit and Systemd, and understand the differences between them.

**Lab Purpose:**
SysVInit and Systemd are two different ways of managing Linux startup processes. SysVInit is considered the "classic" method, while Systemd has supplanted it in many distros today.

**Lab Tool:**
Ubuntu 18.04 (or another distro of your choice)

**Lab Topology:**
A single Linux machine, or virtual machine

**Lab Walkthrough:**

*Task 1:*
Ubuntu 18.04 is one of the distros that has switched to Systemd. However, many SysVInit-based scripts are still present and active:

    ls /etc/init.d

Every file in this directory is a script which starts, stops, checks status, and possibly other features for a given service. You can see which scripts are enabled for which *runlevels* with:

    ls -lR /etc/rc*

Take a look the symlinks listed under /etc/rc5.d. Runlevel 5 is the default boot runlevel, when you're booting normally into a desktop with display manager. Runlevel 0 (under /etc/rc0.d) contains links to the scripts run when your computer is halted.

*Task 2:*

Now run:

```
systemctl list-unit-files --state=enabled
```

These are the services which are enabled at boot within Systemd, and should be mostly distinct from the ones listed under /etc/rc*. Use CTRL + C or q to quit.

While SysVInit relies on standard shell scripts, Systemd uses *unit files* with its own custom format. As just one example, take a look at:

```
cat /lib/systemd/system/rsyslog.service
```

Systemd unit files can have many options. See `man systemd.unit` for more information.

*Task 3:*

Finally, take a look at those system logs with:

```
journalctl -xe
```

Journalctl is Systemd's replacement for the classic syslog. Again, however, Ubuntu still has quite a few logs in classic text format—see /var/log.

**Notes:**

Ubuntu once used Upstart as a replacement for SysVInit. However, that project is currently in maintenance mode and no longer being updated. Ubuntu has migrated to Systemd as a replacement for Upstart.

# LAB 30

# Change Runlevels / Boot Targets and Shutdown or Reboot System: Runlevels and Boot Targets

**Lab Objective:**
Learn how to set and change Linux runlevels and boot targets.

**Lab Purpose:**
The standard Linux *runlevels* are as follows:

- 0: Halt
- 1 (or S): Single-user mode
- 2: Multi-user mode, no networking
- 3: Multi-user mode, with networking
- 4: Unused, or runlevel 3 + display manager
- 5: Unused, or runlevel 3 + display manager
- 6: Reboot

**Lab Tool:**
Ubuntu 18.04 (or another distro of your choice)

**Lab Topology:**
A single Linux machine, or virtual machine

**Lab Walkthrough:**

*Task 1:*
Make sure all of your work is saved. Then, you will enter single-user mode (rescue mode) from the Terminal:

```
sudo telinit 1
```

You will be greeted with a root command prompt—this is the original Linux! As hinted by the name, this mode is typically used for rescue operations. If you ever forget your root password (and the root partition isn't encrypted), this is how you could reset it.

From here, type `reboot` to reboot your machine into a GRUB menu. (See Lab 28 if you cannot see the GRUB boot menu.)

*Task 2:*

From the GRUB boot menu, type 'e' to edit the boot commands. Append 3 to the line beginning with "linux", then hit Ctrl+X to boot.

You should find yourself prompted to log in via command line, rather than the graphical prompt you may be used to. After logging in, you will have a shell just as if you had opened the Terminal application.

Now run `sudo telinit 5` to start the display manager.

You may also use `init` for the same purpose.

**Notes:**

It should be noted that, according to the `telinit` man page in Ubuntu 18.04, "the concept of SysV runlevels is obsolete". In the past, you could also use /etc/inittab to set the default runlevel—this is also removed in Ubuntu 18.04.

# LAB 31

# Change Runlevels / Boot Targets and Shutdown or Reboot System: Systemd and Processes

**Lab Objective:**
Learn how to manage Systemd and properly shutdown/restart services.

**Lab Purpose:**
In this lab you will practice managing running services with Systemd and gracefully stopping and starting processes.

**Lab Tool:**
Ubuntu 18.04 (or another distro of your choice)

**Lab Topology:**
A single Linux machine, or virtual machine

**Lab Walkthrough:**

*Task 1:*
Open the Terminal and run:

```
systemctl status rsyslog
```

You should receive some basic status output showing that the rsyslog service is, indeed, running.

Now: `sudo systemctl restart rsyslog`

Check the logs again and you will see the rsyslog startup messages from just a moment ago.

## Task 2:

Run: `ls /lib/systemd/system`

These are the Systemd unit files (there are a lot). As the equivalent to SysV runlevels, these unit files are symlinked from various *targets* in /etc/systemd/system. Run:

- `ls -l /etc/systemd/system`
- `ls -l /etc/systemd/system/multi-user.target.wants`

## Task 3:

Acpid is an ACPI daemon for managing hardware events, like sleep or hitting the power button. To check whether ACPI is active on your system (it probably is):

```
acpi_available && echo yes || echo no
```

If yes, then you can run `acpi_listen` and hit the power or sleep buttons, or close the screen, to trigger and view ACPI events.

## Notes:

A classic command is called `wall`, which was used to notify users of system maintenance and other events. In practice, it is rarely used anymore, but still present on most Linux systems.

# LAB 32

# Design Hard Disk Layout

**Lab Objective:**
Learn how to design a disk partitioning scheme.

**Lab Purpose:**
In this lab, you will learn about disk partitioning, partition types, and how to set up partitioning using tools such as `fdisk`.

**WARNING:** In this lab, you will begin partitioning your main disk with `fdisk`. As long as you do not use the write command, these changes will stay in memory only and your data will be safe. As an extra precaution, you may wish to run `fdisk` on a secondary drive, or create another VM just for this purpose.

**Lab Tool:**
Ubuntu 18.04 (or another distro of your choice)

**Lab Topology:**
A single Linux machine, or virtual machine

**Lab Walkthrough:**

*Task 1:*
Open the Terminal and run `sudo fdisk /dev/sda`—substitute your hard disk for /dev/sda, if sda is not the right device.

Enter p to see the current partition layout. If you selected your main disk, you should see at least one partition, along with its size, type, and whether it is a boot partition. For example, in the output below:

```
/dev/sda1   *      2048    41940991        41938944        20G     83      Linux
```

The disk contains a single 20GB partition, of type 83—a Linux filesystem (enter l to list all of the types).

*Task 2:*

Now let's delete (again, *from memory only*) any pre-existing partitions. Type d and answer the prompts until none remain.

Then:

- Enter n to add a new partition. This should be a primary partition, number 1, 100M in size. It would be mounted at /boot.
- Repeat this for the swap partition. Make it 4G in size, or double the system RAM. Enter t to change this partition type to 82 (Linux swap). Swap space is "backup RAM" which uses disk as secondary memory if your system runs out of RAM.
- Repeat this for the /var filesystem. Make it 4G in size, or whatever feels right to you based on the disk size.
- Create an extended partition that fills up the rest of the disk. Within this extended partition, you will create partitions for /home and /.
- Create a partition for the /home filesystem. Make it 4G in size, or whatever feels right to you based on the disk size.
- Repeat this for the / filesystem. It will fill up the rest of the disk.
- Enter a to toggle the bootable flag on partition 1.
- Enter p again to see what your results would be.
- **IMPORTANT:** Enter q to quit without writing the partition table.

In most situations, you probably wouldn't need this many partitions, and if you did, you would instead use Logical Volume Manager (LVM). LVM provides a more flexible way of managing logical volumes rather than partitions. In LVM, you would create a *volume group* consisting of one or more physical volumes (disks), and then create logical volumes on top of that in lieu of partitions.

**Notes:**

Some systems contain an EFI System Partition. This would show up in fdisk as a GPT partition, and in general should not be deleted, especially if you have a dual-booting machine.

# LAB 33

## Install a Boot Manager

**Lab Objective:**
Learn how to install and configure a boot manager.

**Lab Purpose:**
In this lab, you will learn about GRUB and how to configure it.

**Lab Tool:**
Ubuntu 18.04 (or another distro of your choice)

**Lab Topology:**
A single Linux machine, or virtual machine

**Lab Walkthrough:**

*Task 1:*
Classically, to edit GRUB configuration you would make changes to grub.cfg, menu.lst, and other files manually. In Ubuntu 18.04, the configurations are auto-generated based on the contents of /etc/grub.d and /etc/default/grub.

Open the Terminal, and with your favorite editor, edit /etc/default/grub:

- Change GRUB_TIMEOUT_STYLE to menu.
- Change GRUB_TIMEOUT to 10 or another value you prefer (in seconds).
- Change GRUB_CMDLINE_LINUX_DEFAULT to "", or experiment with other values for default kernel boot options.
- Change the background by setting GRUB_BACKGROUND to a beautiful image of your choice.
- (See **Answer 1** below if you're struggling to find a working /etc/default/grub file.)
- Finally, close the editor and run `sudo update-grub`

*Task 2:*

Have a peek at /boot/grub/grub.cfg. This is a rather long file, but you should recognize parts of it if you have done Lab 28 and customized GRUB boot commands.

If you are running this on a Linux system that's already fully installed, the next step won't be necessary. However, if you ever wish to boot a secondary disk, you might need to run `grub-install` on that disk. `grub-install` installs GRUB to a disk's *master boot record* (MBR) so that a BIOS can boot it successfully.

*Task 3:*

Finally, reboot your computer/VM and see/hear your shiny new GRUB boot menu. From here you may hit e to edit boot commands or c to enter a command prompt, as in Lab 28.

**Answer 1:**

```
GRUB_DEFAULT=0
GRUB_TIMEOUT_STYLE=menu
GRUB_TIMEOUT=10
GRUB_DISTRIBUTOR=`lsb_release -i -s 2> /dev/null || echo Debian`
GRUB_CMDLINE_LINUX_DEFAULT=""
GRUB_CMDLINE_LINUX=""
GRUB_INIT_TUNE="480 440 1"
# This file must be placed in the /boot/grub directory first
GRUB_BACKGROUND="/boot/grub/image.png"
```

**Notes:**

There have been multiple common bootloaders, including LILO and GRUB Legacy. GRUB2 is the most common and recommended bootloader today.

# LAB 34

# Manage Shared Libraries

**Lab Objective:**
Learn how to identify and install shared libraries.

**Lab Purpose:**
Shared libraries provide common functionality to one or more (often many more) Linux applications. In this lab, you will learn how to manage these very important libraries.

**Lab Tool:**
Ubuntu 18.04 (or another distro of your choice)

**Lab Topology:**
A single Linux machine, or virtual machine

**Lab Walkthrough:**

*Task 1:*
Open the Terminal and run:

```
cat /etc/ld.so.conf{,.d/*}
```

(The above syntax is a shortcut for "/etc/ld.so.conf /etc/ld.so.conf.d/*".)

These files are used to define shared library directories to be used by `ldconfig`. When run as root, `ldconfig` creates links and cache (used when linking a new program) to the most recent libraries in those directories, plus the "trusted" directories of /lib, /usr/lib, /lib64, and /usr/lib64.

*Task 2:*
Now run `ldd $(which passwd)`

This command tells you which shared libraries are linked by the `passwd` tool. The results will vary by implementation, but nearly every program should link to `libc.so.6`, among several others, at a minimum.

Occasionally, if you download software outside of a package manager, you will need to manually install its runtime shared libraries. You can use ldd on a binary file to figure out its dependencies, then search for those dependencies within the package manager.

**Notes:**

You can use the LD_LIBRARY_PATH environment variable, instead of ld.so.conf, to enable additional library directories. However, in most situations, this is not recommended.

# LAB 35

# Use Debian Package Management: Apt

**Lab Objective:**
Learn how to use the Apt package manager to install, upgrade, search for, and uninstall packages.

**Lab Purpose:**
The Apt package manager is a collection of tools meant for Debian-based distros to install and manage DEB-based packages.

**Lab Tool:**
Ubuntu 18.04 (or another distro of your choice)

**Lab Topology:**
A single Linux machine, or virtual machine

**Lab Walkthrough:**

*Task 1:*
Open the Terminal and run:

- `grep -v -e ^# -e ^$ /etc/apt/sources.list`
- `cat /etc/apt/sources.list.d/*`

These files determine which repos will be used by Apt. There are many reputable third-party repos (and many unreputable ones), which you can enable by adding to one of these files, but we'll stick with the defaults for now.

Apt uses a cache that needs to be updated periodically. Do that now with: `sudo apt update`

And then let's run all system updates: `sudo apt -y full-upgrade`

You might not have any updates, even if it's been a while since you've checked:

```
apt list --installed | grep unattended-upgrades
```

Ubuntu 18.04 should come with this package installed and configured by default.

*Task 2:*
Now install a useful package: `sudo apt install apt-file`

Then: `sudo apt-file update`

Now, let's say that you've downloaded the source code for some new and amazing application. Upon attempting to compile it, the code complains that "libvorbis.so" is missing. You can now use `apt-file` to see if there's a package available containing it: `apt-file search libvorbis.so`

It turns out there are several, the most relevant of which being libvorbis-dev (you can run `apt show libvorbis-dev` to confirm that that is the correct package). If you were to install that package, you would then be able to compile your application.

**Notes:**
You may be familiar with the classic tools such as `apt-get` and `apt-cache`. `apt` has not completely superseded those yet, but is more appropriate for interactive usage rather than scripting.

# LAB 36

# Use Debian Package Management: Dpkg

**Lab Objective:**
Learn how to use the dpkg package manager to install, uninstall, and obtain information on packages.

**Lab Purpose:**
Dpkg is a tool for installing Debian-based packages. It does not use repositories nor have automatic dependency resolution like Apt does, but it is useful for managing packages you may have downloaded outside of official repos.

**Lab Tool:**
Ubuntu 18.04 (or another distro of your choice)

**Lab Topology:**
A single Linux machine, or virtual machine

**Lab Walkthrough:**

*Task 1:*
Open the Terminal and run: `dpkg -l`

This lengthy list is, of course, your list of installed packages. To get more information on a given package, try:

- `dpkg -s sudo`
- `dpkg -L sudo`
- `dpkg -p sudo`

Some packages have configuration scripts which can be re-run with:

`sudo dpkg-reconfigure [package]`

To install a package manually, you would download the .deb file and run:

```
sudo dpkg -i [file]
```

Though, again, you would have to also install the dependencies manually first. To remove the package when you're done with it: `dpkg -P [package]`

**Notes:**

Though `dpkg` is great for information gathering, in practice it is generally better to manage your installed packages through a single central database. That may mean adding a third-party repo, or downloading a package and then manually adding it to Apt.

# LAB 37

# Use RPM and YUM Package Management: YUM

**Lab Objective:**
Learn how to use the YUM package manager to install, upgrade, search for, and uninstall packages.

**Lab Purpose:**
The YUM package manager is a collection of tools meant for RedHat-based distros to install and manage RPM-based packages.

> **IMPORTANT:** YUM is not pre-installed with Ubuntu and it may not install correctly. In that case, we recommend setting up another VM with a RedHat-based distro, such as CentOS.

**Lab Tool:**
A RedHat-based distro such as CentOS. Ubuntu is not recommended for this lab.

**Lab Topology:**
A single Linux machine, or virtual machine

**Lab Walkthrough:**

*Task 1:*
Open the Terminal and run:

- `grep -r -v -e ^# -e ^$ /etc/yum.conf{,.d/*}`
- `cat /etc/yum.repos.d/*`

These files determine which repos will be used by YUM. There are many reputable third-party repos (and many unreputable ones), which you can enable by adding to one of these files, but we'll stick with the defaults for now.

Let's start by running all system updates: `sudo yum -y update`

If you chose Fedora, you will be using a newer tool: `sudo dnf -y update`

DNF is a newer tool which is replacing YUM in some distros. If you have one of these distros, you can safely replace all instances of `yum` with `dnf` in this lab.

*Task 2:*
Let's say that you've downloaded the source code for some new and amazing application. Upon attempting to compile it, the code complains that "libvorbis.so" is missing. You can look to see if there's a package available containing it: `yum provides */libvorbis.so`

It turns out there are several, the most relevant of which being libvorbis-devel (you can run `yum info libvorbis-devel` to confirm that that is the correct package). If you were to install that package with `sudo yum -y install libvorbis-devel`, you would then be able to compile your application.

**Notes:**
To experiment with a third major package manager, called Zypper, it is suggested to use a third distro, called OpenSUSE. This is outside the scope of this lab, but if you use Zypper after using Apt and YUM you will likely find that the commands and syntax are quite familiar.

# LAB 38

## Use RPM and YUM Package Management: RPM

**Lab Objective:**
Learn how to use the RPM package manager to install, uninstall, and obtain information on packages.

**Lab Purpose:**
RPM is a tool for installing RPM-based packages. It does not use repositories nor have automatic dependency resolution like YUM does, but it is useful for managing packages you may have downloaded outside of official repos.

**IMPORTANT:** RPM is not pre-installed with Ubuntu and it may not install correctly. In that case, we recommend setting up another VM with a RedHat-based distro, such as CentOS.

**Lab Tool:**
A RedHat-based distro such as CentOS. Ubuntu is not recommended for this lab.

**Lab Topology:**
A single Linux machine, or virtual machine

**Lab Walkthrough:**

*Task 1:*
Open the Terminal and run: `rpm -qa`

This lengthy list is, of course, your list of installed packages. To get more information on a given package, try:

- `rpm -qs sudo`
- `rpm -q --dump sudo`

To install a package manually, you would run:

`sudo rpm -i [file]`, where `[file]` can be either a downloaded .rpm or a URL. Again, though, you would have to also install the dependencies manually first. To remove the package when you're done with it: `rpm -e [package]`

## *Task 2:*

Another useful tool is `rpm2cpio`. This tool converts a .rpm file into a cpio archive and spits it out on stdout. This makes it easy to access the files within, independent of RPM. For example:

`rpm2cpio package.rpm | cpio -dium`

**Notes:**

Though `rpm` is great for information gathering, in practice it is generally better to manage your installed packages through a single central database. That may mean adding a third-party repo, or downloading a package and then manually adding it to YUM/DNF.

# LAB 39

## Linux as a Virtualization Guest

**Lab Objective:**
Learn how to manage Linux desktops and servers in the context of virtualization.

**Lab Purpose:**
If you've followed the labs in order, you are probably running this lab in a VM. In addition to desktop virtualization, with the advent of "cloud computing" and IaaS, server virtualization has become a large part of everyday life for a professional Linux administrator.

**Lab Tool:**
Ubuntu 18.04 (or another distro of your choice)

**Lab Topology:**
A single Linux virtual machine running on VirtualBox

**Lab Walkthrough:**

*Task 1:*
Open the VirtualBox Settings for the VM you are using for this lab. If possible, beef up the VM by doing the following (or if you don't have the system resources, then shrink resources assigned to the VM instead):

- Assign additional RAM and an additional processor to the VM
- Create another virtual disk image and assign it to the VM
- Assign an additional network adapter to the VM

Now reboot the VM and look to see if you can detect the additional resources. Does the memory show up in `free`? Can you see an extra processor with `lscpu`? Does `lsblk` show another disk? What about the network with `ip link show`?

The point of this exercise is to learn how easy it is to change the resources of a virtualized computer compared with a physical one. The same is true in the server world.

## Task 2:

In VirtualBox, make a clone of this VM. Boot it, access the Terminal, and run: `ip addr show`

Compare the results with the original VM. Are the IP address and MAC address the same, or were they automatically changed? (Depending on your settings, either could be the case.)

In a cloud scenario of multiple machines being cloned onto the same network, it is critical to make sure the network information is unique for each instance. This is also true of some security-related information, such as SSH host keys and the D-Bus machine ID.

## Task 3:

Finally, it is important to understand that guest VM's must have certain features beyond a generic Linux installation to make them usable as VM's. To illustrate this, run:

    lsmod | grep vbox

You may see several VirtualBox-related kernel modules, such as `vboxguest`, `vboxsf`, or `vboxvideo`, among others. Additionally, specific kernel configuration is required: `grep GUEST /boot/config*`

**Notes:**
Cloud-init is a package commonly used in cloud server environments to handle the unique per-server configuration on the first boot of an image deployment.

# LAB 40

## Work on the Command Line: Commands and Quoting

**Lab Objective:**
Learn basic Linux commands and shell syntax.

**Lab Purpose:**
The Bash command shell is pre-installed on millions of Linux computers around the world. Understanding how this shell works is a critical skill for working with Linux.

**Lab Tool:**
Ubuntu 18.04 (or another distro of your choice)

**Lab Topology:**
A single Linux machine, or virtual machine

**Lab Walkthrough:**

*Task 1:*
Open the Terminal application, then enter: `echo Hello World`

The `echo` command simply prints out all of the "words," or arguments, that you give to it. This might not seem very useful, until…

*Task 2:*
Now enter the following four commands, in order:

```
quote='cat /etc/issue'
backquote=`cat /etc/issue`
echo $quote
echo $backquote
```

Here, `quote` and `backquote` are called *variables*. In the first two lines, we set them to the values `'cat /etc/issue'` and `` `cat /etc/issue` ``, respectively. (We'll get to the difference between quotes and backquotes in a minute.) In the last two lines, we reference the variables by putting `$` before them, and print out their contents.

## Task 3:

To understand single quotes, double quotes, and backquotes, enter the following:

```
hello="echo hello"
echo "$hello"
echo '$hello'
echo `$hello`
```

Double quotes allow for variables to have their values referenced. Single quotes are always literal, while backquotes *execute* the command (including variable references) within those quotes.

## Task 4:

Now run the following commands:

- `pwd`
- `which pwd`
- `uname -a`

Can you figure out what these commands do? If not, there's another command—`man`—which could help you get some information.

Run `set -v`, then run the above commands again. You've just set the verbose flag in Bash, which repeats every command as you run it. To unset it, just run `unset -v` ...

Just kidding! The completely unintuitive way to *unset* the `-v` flag is to `set +v`—run `set --help` to get more information on what Bash has available for customization; there's quite a bit.

`unset` actually has a different purpose, which is to unset variables. Observe:

- `foo=123`
- `echo $foo`
- `unset foo`
- `echo $foo`

**Notes:**

In some cases, you will want to reference variables with the `${variable}` syntax. This is equivalent to `$variable`, but the reasons for choosing one over the other are beyond the scope of this lab.

## Lab 40–Work on the Command Line: Commands and Quoting

Backquotes also have an alternative syntax:

```
$(echo hello)
```

This syntax is generally preferred over backquotes. We only mention backquotes to distinguish them from single quotes and ensure the differences are clear.

# LAB 41

# Work on the Command Line: Environment Variables, Types, and History

**Lab Objective:**
Learn about Bash environment variables, types, and how to use the shell history.

**Lab Purpose:**
The Bash command shell is pre-installed on millions of Linux computers around the world. Understanding how this shell works is a critical skill for working with Linux.

**Lab Tool:**
Ubuntu 18.04 (or another distro of your choice)

**Lab Topology:**
A single Linux machine, or virtual machine

**Lab Walkthrough:**

*Task 1:*
Open the Terminal application, then enter: `echo $PATH`

The PATH environment variable lists all locations that Bash will search when you enter a command with a *relative* path. A *relative* path example is `bash`, compared to `/bin/bash`, which is an *absolute* path.

There are other environment variables as well. You can view all of them, and their values, using the `env` command.

*Task 2:*
You can add or modify an environment variable with `export`. For example:

    export PATH=${PATH}:./

In most cases, this change will disappear when you exit Bash, but the advantage of `export` is that child processes will now be able to see the new/modified variable.

For example:

- `foo=123`
- `export bar=456`
- `bash`
- `echo $foo $bar`

This prints `456` because only `bar` is seen by the child shell.

*Task 3:*
Another useful Bash command is called `type`. Use `type` to figure out information on other commands or functions:

```
type -a date
type -a if
type -a echo
type -a ls
```

`type` will tell you if a command/shell function is a binary file (like /bin/date), a shell built-in (like `help`), an alias (which you can view with `alias`), or a shell keyword (like `if` or `while`).

*Task 4:*
Enter `history` to see a history of commands you have typed into Bash.

To repeat a command, simply enter ! and then the appropriate number. For example. !12 will execute command #12 in the history list.

If you accidentally saved a password or other sensitive information to the history, you may use, for example, `history -d 47` to delete command #47 from the list, or even `history -c` to clear the history altogether.

If you want to save your current shell's history to another file, use `history -w filename`

The default filename Bash saves its history to is .bash_history. However, by default, it only saves at the end of a session. If your session crashes, or you open multiple sessions, etc., then your shell history could become incomplete or out of order.

**Notes:**
If you wish to permanently modify an environment variable or other shell setting, look into the `.bashrc` and `.bash_profile` files.

# LAB 42

# Process Text Streams Using Filters

**Lab Objective:**
Learn how to use small text filtering programs to obtain command output.

**Lab Purpose:**
In this lab, you will send text files and output through a number of utility commands.

**Lab Tool:**
Ubuntu 18.04 (or another distro of your choice)

**Lab Topology:**
A single Linux machine, or virtual machine

**Lab Walkthrough:**

*Task 1:*
Open the Terminal and run:

```
echo "foo
BAR
Baz
Quux123
456plugh
7xy8zz9y0
Hello
goodbyE" | nl -n ln > lab42.txt
```

Here, you are creating a simple text file—when piped through `nl`, the file is created with line numbers. Use `cat` and `less` to check the file's contents.

*Task 2:*
`head` and `tail` are useful for obtaining only the first or last n lines of a file:

- `head -3 lab42.txt`
- `tail -3 lab42.txt`

## Task 3:

Now you will get *hashes* of this file. Hashing uses one-way algorithms to verify the integrity of files (or passwords); if the hashes of two files match, then those files are theoretically identical. Get the MD5, SHA256, and SHA512 hashes, respectively:

- `md5sum lab42.txt`
- `sha256sum lab42.txt`
- `sha512sum lab42.txt`

The output from those three commands should be, respectively:

```
e18bce7fb26d0394587e6692106c99b3  lab42.txt
970468127af90d4e4eed6fd7e85461bcf02ac49910959fccb2179c2bc5e41d87  lab42.txt
9fd0c523be2951ecd683e53b79feceecb804aaa31bdf2906b5458268794ff5f85bbd2f6ecdd944bb68693d65ac39c23c69438d23b43d3060f413aa240c13a629  lab42.txt
```

If your hashes don't match, you may have a typo!

## Task 4:

`cut` is a useful tool to obtain only the fields you want from structured flat files. For example, compare the difference in output between these two commands:

- `cut -f1 lab42.txt`
- `cut -f2 lab42.txt`

The first command lists the line numbers, while the second lists only the words.

You can use `sort` to sort the output in various ways; for example, by reversing it:

```
sort -r lab42.txt
```

There's also a command called `uniq` which can ignore or count duplicate instances of some line or field. (`sort` also has the `-u` switch to do this in a single step).

Sometimes, you may also need to obtain a byte-level representation of a file in octal or other format. This can be useful if a file contains characters which are not readable by your terminal:

```
od lab42.txt
```

## Lab 42—Process Text Streams Using Filters

Finally, use `wc` to count characters, words, and lines:

- `wc -c lab42.txt`
- `wc -w lab42.txt`
- `wc -l lab42.txt`

Did you get 109, 16, and 8, respectively?

### Task 5:
Now you will use the `tr` filter to modify the output and replace all digits with underscores:

`cat lab42.txt | tr [0-9] _`

`sed` is another more complicated, but more featureful, way of accomplishing this same task:

`sed 's/[0-9]/_/g' lab42.txt`

A full discussion of `sed` syntax is outside the scope of this lab, but it can do far more than `tr` alone and is a tool well worth learning.

Finally, split this file into four more files of two lines each:

- `split -l2 lab42.txt lab42`
- `ls lab42*`
- `cat lab42aa`

### Task 6:
Now clean up with: `rm lab42*`

### Notes:
In addition to `cat`, you can also view the contents of compressed files directly. Use `zcat`, `bzcat`, or `xzcat`, for gzipped, bzipped, or LZMA formats, respectively.

# LAB 43

## Perform Basic File Management: Files and Directories

**Lab Objective:**
Learn how to copy, move, and manage larger numbers of files and directories.

**Lab Purpose:**
In this lab, you will learn how to manage files and directories, including recursively.

**Lab Tool:**
Ubuntu 18.04 (or another distro of your choice)

**Lab Topology:**
A single Linux machine, or virtual machine

**Lab Walkthrough:**

*Task 1:*
Open the Terminal application, then enter:

```
mkdir lab43
cd lab43
touch f1 f2 f3
```

You now have a single directory containing three empty files.

*Task 2:*

```
cp f1 f4
ls
```

As expected, the `cp` command has created a fourth empty file. However, what happens when you do the following?

```
cp f1 f3
```

The f3 file gets overwritten—hope you didn't have any important data in there!

To prevent this, use either the -i or -n flag. -i stands for *interactive*, which means you will be prompted before overwriting. -n stands for *no-clobber*, which means the target file will never be overwritten. However, cp won't warn you about this, so -i is recommended for general shell usage.

*Task 3:*
Now run:

```
mv f1 f5
```

mv is the move command, so this does what you might expect, effectively renaming f1 to f5. Like cp, mv also has -i and -n flags, which have the same effects.

*Task 4:*
Now run:

```
mkdir foo bar
mv f2 foo
mv f3 foo
mv f* bar
```

What do you predict the final directory structure will look like? Now check it with ls -aR bar—did it match your prediction? (See **Answer 1** below.)

What you did with f* is called *globbing*. That command matched every file *and* directory starting with f (but not F—like everything else in Linux, globbing is case-sensitive), so f4, f5, and foo were all moved into bar.

*Task 5:*
Copy foo back to the current directory, with cp bar/foo ./

… Whoops! What happened? In order to copy a directory with its contents, you must use the -r flag (for *recursive*): cp -r bar/foo ./

*Task 6:*
Finally, let's clean up:

```
cd ~
rm -r lab43
```

## Lab 43—Perform Basic File Management: Files and Directories

**Answer 1:**
```
bar:
.    ..      f4      f5      foo

bar/foo:
.    ..      f2      f3
```

**Notes:**
Be careful with `rm -r`—that command removes an entire directory without prompting you. Many horror stories can be found on the internet of people inadvertently deleting important files when they weren't paying attention!

# LAB 44

## Perform Basic File Management: Find and Globbing

**Lab Objective:**
Learn how to use advanced filename expansion in Bash, as well as the `find` command to locate and act on specific files.

**Lab Purpose:**
In this lab, you will learn about shell globbing, and how to use the `find` command to locate files based on type, size, etc. and execute commands on those files.

**Lab Tool:**
Ubuntu 18.04 (or another distro of your choice)

**Lab Topology:**
A single Linux machine, or virtual machine

**Lab Walkthrough:**

*Task 1:*
It is important to understand that, although shell globbing shares some commonalities with regular expressions, Bash itself does not recognize the full regex syntax. Instead, Bash simply recognizes and expands wild cards.

Open the Terminal and run:

- `mkdir lab44`
- `cd lab44`
- `touch a1 a2 a12 b1 b2 b12 c1 c2 c12`

*Task 2:*
To understand how advanced globbing works, run the following commands and observe the output (on the right):

- `ls a?`         a1    a2

- `ls a*`            a1    a12    a2
- `ls [ab]?`         a1    a2     b1    b2
- `ls [ab]*`         a1    a12    a2    b1    b12    b2
- `ls [^ab]*`        c1    c12    c2
- `ls ?[1-2]`        a1    a2     b1    b2    c1     c2
- `ls ?[1-2]*`       a1    a12    a2    b1    b12    b2
  c1    c12    c2

*Task 3:*
Now, apply this shell globbing to find and execute a command on a certain set of files (copy and paste won't work for the below):

    find . -name "c?" -execdir ls -l {} \;

What this command is doing is searching in the current directory (recursively) for all files named "c?", which in this case matches c1 and c2. It then effectively executes `ls -l [file]` on each file found. The {} syntax references the filename, while the escaped semicolon denotes the end of arguments to the `ls` command.

Experiment further with `find`:

- `sudo find / -not -type l -perm -o+w`
- `sudo find / -perm -u+s -user root -type f`

Both of the above commands are useful for security auditing purposes. The first one searches for (non-symlink) world-writable files. The second one searches for files which are "setuid root," or in other words, run with root permissions by a non-root user.

*Task 4:*
Clean up:

- `cd ..`
- `rm -r lab44`

**Notes:**
Another useful command is `file`, which tells you a given file's type. Can you figure out how to use `file` in combination with find to locate all text files within your home directory?

# LAB 45

# Perform Basic File Management: Archiving and Unarchiving

**Lab Objective:**
Learn how to create, extract, and examine various types of archive files.

**Lab Purpose:**
In this lab, you will learn about gzip, bzip2, and xz compressed archives—as well as two tools, `tar` and `cpio`, to manage most Linux archive types.

**Lab Tool:**
Ubuntu 18.04 (or another distro of your choice)

**Lab Topology:**
A single Linux machine, or virtual machine

**Lab Walkthrough:**

*Task 1:*
Open the Terminal application and run the following:

```
mkdir lab45
cd lab45
touch f1 f2 f3 f4 f5 f6 f7 f8 f9
```

*Task 2:*
Though ZIP is a common format and well-supported on Linux, it is not the main compression format Linux uses. That would be the classic gzip:

```
gzip f*
ls
```

Wait a minute... why are there now nine gzipped files instead of just one? And what happened to the originals?

This is why gzip is considered a *compression* format rather than an *archive* one. To create a single, easy-to-use archive file, we need a different tool...

## Task 3:
Run: `tar -cf files.tar.gz f*`

Now, with the help of the *tar archiver*, you have your gzipped archive in files.tar.gz... well, sort of.

Normally, with a gzipped tarball, you would be able to extract it with `tar -xf files.tar.gz` and get all of the original files back. Instead, you could try that yourself now, and you would get the nine .gz files.

There's a better way. Let's blow this up and start over:

```
rm f*
touch f1 f2 f3 f4 f5 f6 f7 f8 f9
tar -czf archive.tar.gz f*
tar --list -f archive.tar.gz
```

Ta-da! Now you see a list of nine files within your single compressed tarball.

## Task 4:
gzip isn't the only format you can use with `tar`:

```
tar -cjf archive.tar.bz2 f*
tar -cJf archive.tar.xz f*
```

The bzip2 and XZ formats, respectively, are newer and use different algorithms from gzip, but the end result is the same. `tar` can extract all of its formats in the same way, simply by using `tar -xf filename`.

## Task 5:
`cpio` is another archiving tool used, most notably, in the RPM package manager and `initramfs`. Run:

- `find . | cpio -o > lab45.cpio`
- `cpio -t < lab45.cpio`
- `rm f1`
- `cpio -i -d f1 < lab45.cpio`
- `rm f*`
- `cpio -i -vd < lab45.cpio`

## LAB 45–PERFORM BASIC FILE MANAGEMENT: ARCHIVING AND UNARCHIVING

In short, what you are doing here is creating an archive, listing that archive (with `-t`), extracting the f1 file, and then extracting all of the files.

*Task 6:*

Another useful command for backups is `dd`. Typically this is used for block-level copying of an entire disk or partition, but it can also be used with ordinary files:

```
dd if=f1 of=f1.bak
```

Of course, if that's all you were doing, you could just use `cp`. A more typical usage would be something like (**do not actually run this**):

```
dd if=/dev/sda1 of=/dev/sdb1
```

Assuming you had already connected a backup drive, this would copy the entire /dev/sda1 partition onto it.

*Task 7:*

Finally, clean up:

```
cd ~
rm -r lab45
```

**Notes:**

To use compression-only without `tar` for archiving, each format has its own compression and decompression commands. Use `gzip/gunzip`, `bzip2/bunzip2`, and `xz/unxz`, for gzip, bzip2, and LZMA formats, respectively.

# LAB 46

# Use Streams, Pipes, and Redirects: Redirection and File Descriptors

**Lab Objective:**
Learn how to redirect input and output in Bash.

**Lab Purpose:**
Bash has a commonly-used feature, known as I/O redirection, that makes life easier when using Linux. In this lab, you will learn how to make use of this powerful feature.

**Lab Tool:**
Ubuntu 18.04 (or another distro of your choice)

**Lab Topology:**
A single Linux machine, or virtual machine

**Lab Walkthrough:**

*Task 1:*
Open the Terminal application and run:

```
mkdir lab46
cd lab46
echo "hello world" > hello
cat hello
```

You just *redirected* the output from your `echo` command into the hello file. The > is a shortcut; the proper version of this would be 1>, where 1 is called a *file descriptor*, which references the *standard output*.

*Task 2:*
Now run:

```
ls nonexistent 2>> hello
cat hello
```

Based on the new contents of the hello file ("ls: cannot access 'nonexistent': No such file or directory"), what can you surmise about the function of 2>>? Here, 2 is a file descriptor for *standard error*.

*Task 3:*
Sometimes, you want to redirect both output *and* error to the same place. In ye olden days, you would have to do something ugly like this: `ls foo > bar 2>&1`

However, modern versions of Bash have an easy-to-use shortcut: `ls foo &> bar`

*Task 4:*
We've talked about redirecting output, but what about input? To learn about that, run the following commands:

```
cat < hello

read foo <<< "foo"
echo $foo

cat << END-OF-FILE > goodbye
hello
goodbye
END-OF-FILE
cat goodbye
```

In short: < redirects input from a file name, << starts a here document, and <<< redirects input from another command.

*Task 5:*
You can also create your own file descriptors. Observe:

- exec 3<> foo
- echo "Hello World" >&3
- cat foo
- exec 3>&-
- echo "fail" >&3

What this is doing is opening file descriptor 3 (for both reading and writing), with the file foo, and sending output to that. The fourth line then closes the file descriptor, causing the last `echo` command to fail.

## Lab 46–Use Streams, Pipes, and Redirects: Redirection and File Descriptors

*Task 6:*

Finally, clean up:

```
cd ~
rm -r lab46
```

**Notes:**

To open a file descriptor for reading only, you could use `exec 3< file`, or for writing only, `exec 3> file`.

# LAB 47

# Use Streams, Pipes, and Redirects: Pipes

**Lab Objective:**
Learn how to use pipes in Bash to use the output of one command as the input of another.

**Lab Purpose:**
Bash has a commonly-used feature, known as pipes, that makes life easier when using Linux. In this lab, you will learn how to make use of this powerful feature.

**Lab Tool:**
Ubuntu 18.04 (or another distro of your choice)

**Lab Topology:**
A single Linux machine, or virtual machine

**Lab Walkthrough:**

*Task 1:*
Pipes (|) let you use the output of a command as the input to another command. In many situations (but not all), | and <<< are kind of a reverse of one another. For example, the output of...

```
echo "hello
world" | grep e
```

... is identical to the output of...

```
grep e <<< "hello
world"
```

Try to predict the output of the following command string before you run it (see **Answer 1** below):

```
grep non hello | cut -d: -f3
```

## Task 2:

In Lab 46, you learned how to redirect command output. Now run:

```
echo "Hello World" | tee hello
cat hello
```

What's going on here? The `tee` command redirects output to a file while also sending it to stdout. You can use a special `|&` pipe to redirect both stdout and stderr:

```
rm hello
ls hello |& tee hello
cat hello
```

`tee` also has a `-a` switch to append to the file rather than overwriting it.

## Task 3:

While a pipe passes the output of a command as the input of another command, `xargs` passes the output of a command as the *argument(s)* of another command:

```
echo hello | xargs cat
rm hello
```

The `xargs` man page describes a number of useful arguments, including setting a delimiter and forcing interactive prompting for each argument.

**Answer 1:**

```
No such file or directory
```

**Notes:**

Challenge: Chain together a series of commands that uses each of: pipes, `ls`, `xargs`, and at least one redirection.

# LAB 48

# Create, Monitor, and Kill Processes: Foreground and Background Jobs

**Lab Objective:**
Learn how to run jobs in the foreground and background.

**Lab Purpose:**
Sometimes, you want to run a process in Linux and then walk away, or hide the job in the background so you don't see it. In this lab, you will learn how to do that.

**Lab Tool:**
Ubuntu 18.04 (or another distro of your choice)

**Lab Topology:**
A single Linux machine, or virtual machine

**Lab Walkthrough:**

*Task 1:*
Open the Terminal and run `sleep 10000`, then press Ctrl+Z. Now run:

- `jobs`
- `bg`
- `jobs`
- `fg`

Hit Ctrl+C to cancel the sleep job.

When you first ran the `sleep` command and then pressed Ctrl+Z, that command was *stopped* (although the term "stopped" may be misleading—"paused" is more accurate). When stopped, a job is no longer running, ticking down seconds, or whatever it's supposed to be doing. The `bg` command changes that, making the job run in the background. You can see the list of running jobs with `jobs`, and bring the most recent background job into the foreground with `fg`. Note that you can run `fg` on stopped jobs as well, you don't have to start them running first.

To run a task in the background directly, simply append a &, like: `sleep 10000 &`

*Task 2:*
Run `sleep 10000 &`, then exit your terminal completely by closing the window (do not use the `exit` command).

When you open a new terminal, run `ps -ef | grep sleep` and you should find that your sleep process has terminated. To keep a job running even after closing a shell session, run the command under `nohup`:

```
nohup sleep 10000 &
```

If you exit the terminal now and come back, you will still find that process running. `nohup` causes a command to ignore what's called the *hangup* signal.

*Task 3:*
At times, you may need to run a normal foreground process, but still have it running even after you have walked away. This is more common on servers, where an admin will connect via OpenSSH and wants to decouple a running process from their own shell, while still monitoring for problems.

There are two tools, screen and tmux, which can help with this, but on a default setup you'll need to install them first: `sudo apt -y install screen tmux`

`screen` and `tmux` operate slightly differently, but the principles are the same. Start with `screen`:

- `screen`
- `i=0; while true; do i=$(($i+1)); echo $i; sleep 1; done`

Now hit Ctrl+A, followed by D. These keystrokes will detach from your `screen` session and return to your shell. You can view these sessions with `screen -list`. Now:

- `tmux`
- `j=0; while true; do j=$(($j+1)); echo $j; sleep 1; done`

Now hit Ctrl+B, followed by D. Again, this will detach from the session and put you back at the shell, but your process is still running. You view these sessions with `tmux ls`.

Finally, return to each session, respectively, with `screen -x` and `tmux attach`. (Hit Ctrl+C and run `exit` in between them to terminate the processes.) If there is more than one

## Lab 48–Create, Monitor, and Kill Processes: Foreground and Background Jobs

session, you will be prompted to choose one, otherwise the command will reattach to the running session.

**Notes:**

`screen` and `tmux` have a variety of options, comparable to text editors in some respects. Neither of them is "better," but you might want to explore both tools and decide which you prefer.

# LAB 49

## Create, Monitor, and Kill Processes: Process Monitoring

**Lab Objective:**
Learn how to monitor processes and their resource usage.

**Lab Purpose:**
In this lab, you will learn how to monitor a number of metrics for both foreground and background processes.

**Lab Tool:**
Ubuntu 18.04 (or another distro of your choice)

**Lab Topology:**
A single Linux machine, or virtual machine

**Lab Walkthrough:**

*Task 1:*
If you weren't careful to terminate all of your sleep processes from Lab 48, you might have a stray or two running. Let's find out:

```
ps -ef
```

Well, that's a lot of output! You could maybe filter it through a | `grep sleep` or use `ps` without arguments, but there's a better way:

```
pgrep -a sleep
```

`pgrep` supports regex and has a number of matching options to make sure you find the right process(es).

*Task 2:*

A `sleep` process isn't going to use many system resources, but plenty of other processes might. It's important to know how to monitor those.

Take a look at `free -h`. This gives you an output of system memory usage. The most generally useful columns here are "total", "used", and "available." The "available" column offers an estimate of memory which is free for starting new processes without swapping. That isn't the same as "free" memory, which is often low on Linux systems. This is because the OS can take advantage of this memory for performance reasons, while still holding it as "available" for user processes.

`free` has a `-s N` switch to automatically print the output every N seconds. That's useful in its own right, but wouldn't you like to have that ability for every command? Then `watch` might be for you! `free -h -s 10` is equivalent to `watch -n 10 free -h`.

Finally, take a look at the `top` command. Running `top` opens a rather confusing output screen that's continually changing, but one of its most useful capabilities may be simply sorting processes by CPU or memory usage. When in `top`, use the < and > keys to shift the sorting column over to the metric you're interested in. In the upper panel, you can also see the system load, a count of running processes, and some CPU and memory metrics. Finally, press 'q' to quit.

It is strongly recommended to spend some time reading the `top` man page, as this is one of the most featureful system monitoring tools that is installed by default.

**Notes:**
`uptime`, despite the name, is another quick way to get system load. However, `top` also shows this, as well as lots of other useful information.

# LAB 50

## Create, Monitor, and Kill Processes: Sending Signals

**Lab Objective:**
Learn how to send signals to processes in Linux.

**Lab Purpose:**
In this lab, you will learn about signals, including but not limited to kill, and how to send them to processes.

**Lab Tool:**
Ubuntu 18.04 (or another distro of your choice)

**Lab Topology:**
A single Linux machine, or virtual machine

**Lab Walkthrough:**

*Task 1:*
Sometimes, in Linux, things are not quite as they seem. This sequence of commands will demonstrate that:

- `sleep 10000 &`
- `kill -19 $(pgrep sleep)`
- `jobs`
- `kill -18 $(pgrep sleep)`
- `jobs`

What is happening here? Contrary to its name, the `kill` command doesn't necessarily kill processes. Instead, it sends them a *signal*, which may or may not be SIGKILL, the signal that immediately terminates a process. In fact, by default, `kill` doesn't even send SIGKILL—it sends SIGTERM (terminate gracefully), which is basically a computer's way of saying "please wrap up everything that you're doing… or else I'll have to send SIGKILL."

In this sequence, you first sent signal 19, which is SIGSTOP (stop), followed by signal 18, which is SIGCONT (continue). Given the output of `jobs`, this should now make more sense.

You can see a list of all signals with `kill -L`

*Task 2:*
Now create a few sleep processes if you haven't already, and use either `killall` or `pkill` to terminate them all with a single command. Both commands have the same general function, with slightly different arguments, so it's worth experimenting with and reading the man pages for both.

**Notes:**
`pkill` and `pgrep` have exactly the same searching/matching semantics. This means you can use `pgrep` as a "dry run" to find the processes you want to signal before actually doing so.

# LAB 51

## Modify Process Execution Priorities

**Lab Objective:**
Learn how to manage the priority of started and running processes.

**Lab Purpose:**
In this lab, you will learn how to get a running task's priority, change its priority, and set the priority of a task to be run.

**Lab Tool:**
Ubuntu 18.04 (or another distro of your choice)

**Lab Topology:**
A single Linux machine, or virtual machine

**Lab Walkthrough:**

*Task 1:*
Open the Terminal and run the following commands:

- `nice -n 19 sleep 10000 &`
- `ps -l`
- `sudo renice -n -20 $(pgrep sleep)`
- `ps -l`
- `pkill sleep`

What you've done here is started a `sleep` process with a "niceness" value of 19. This is the most "nice" a process can be—in other words, the least demanding in terms of priority. Then you changed its priority, with `renice`, to the "meanest" possible value of -20, or the most demanding in terms of priority. The default priority for all user processes is 0, and you must be root to run a process with higher priority. `ps -l` will list your running processes with their priorities.

**Notes:**
You can also use `top` to list and sort processes by their priority values.

# LAB 52

# Search Text Files Using Regular Expressions: Basic Regex

**Lab Objective:**
Learn how to use basic regular expressions for complex string pattern matching.

**Lab Purpose:**
Regular expressions are a tool used commonly in Linux to match complex patterns in strings and text files. Many tools support regular expressions. With basic regex, some metacharacters require backslashes in front of them.

**Lab Tool:**
Ubuntu 18.04 (or another distro of your choice)

**Lab Topology:**
A single Linux machine, or virtual machine

**Lab Walkthrough:**

*Task 1:*
Open the Terminal application and create a text file first (copy and paste won't work for the below):

```
echo "abc123
456def
<html>
Hello World!
password
01234567890
A1B2C3D4E5
6F7G8H9I0J
Quoth the raven: 'Nevermore.'" > lab52.txt
```

## Task 2:

Now, try to predict what the output of each command will be before running it (see **Answers 1-7** below):

- `grep [0-3] lab52.txt`
- `grep [e68] lab52.txt`
- `grep "^[0-9a-zA-Z]\+$" lab52.txt`
- `grep "[0-9][A-Z]\?[0-9]" lab52.txt`
- `grep "<\|:" lab52.txt`
- `grep -v ".*" lab52.txt`
- `fgrep -v ".*" lab52.txt`

That last command is a bit of a curveball. `fgrep` (short for `grep -F`) treats an expression as a literal string and does not use regex matching. So it is excluding all matches containing a literal '.*'—which, of course, is none of them.

### Answer 1:

```
abc123
01234567890
A1B2C3D4E5
6F7G8H9I0J
```

### Answer 2:

```
456def
Hello World!
01234567890
6F7G8H9I0J
Quoth the raven: 'Nevermore.'
```

### Answer 3:

```
abc123
456def
password
01234567890
A1B2C3D4E5
6F7G8H9I0J
```

### Answer 4:

```
abc123
456def
1234567890
```

## Lab 52–Search Text Files Using Regular Expressions: Basic Regex

```
A1B2C3D4E5
6F7G8H9IOJ
```

### Answer 5:

```
<html>
Quoth the raven: 'Nevermore.'
```

### Answer 6:

(No output)

### Answer 7:

```
abc123
456def
<html>
Hello World!
password
01234567890
A1B2C3D4E5
6F7G8H9IOJ
Quoth the raven: 'Nevermore.'
```

### Notes:

**Regexr** is a great resource for practicing your regular expressions. See `man 7 regex` for more information on regex as supported by your distro.

# LAB 53

# Search Text Files Using Regular Expressions: Extended Regex

**Lab Objective:**
Learn how to use extended regular expressions for complex string pattern matching.

**Lab Purpose:**
Regular expressions are a tool used commonly in Linux to match complex patterns in strings and text files. Many tools support regular expressions. With extended regex, metacharacters do not require backslashes.

**Lab Tool:**
Ubuntu 18.04 (or another distro of your choice)

**Lab Topology:**
A single Linux machine, or virtual machine

**Lab Walkthrough:**

*Task 1:*
Open the Terminal application and create a text file first:

```
echo "abc123
456def
<html>
Hello World!
password
01234567890
A1B2C3D4E5
6F7G8H9I0J
Quoth the raven: 'Nevermore.'" > lab53.txt
```

# LPIC1 Linux Administrator–Exam 101

*Task 2:*

Now, try to predict what the output of each command will be before running it (see **Answers 1-7** below):

- egrep [0-3] lab53.txt
- egrep [e68] lab53.txt
- egrep "^[0-9a-zA-Z]+$" lab53.txt
- egrep "[0-9][A-Z]?[0-9]" lab53.txt
- egrep "<|:" lab53.txt
- egrep -v ".*" lab53.txt
- egrep "[ls]{2}" lab53.txt

egrep (short for grep -E) uses extended regex, instead of basic regex, which is the default.

*Task 3:*

Finally, apply some of what you've learned about regex to these sed substitution commands. Again, what will the output be (see **Answers 8-10** below)?

- sed -E 's/[A-Z]/_/g' lab53.txt
- sed -E 's/^[a-z]+$/[omitted]/' lab53.txt
- sed -E 's/([a-z])\1/**/g' lab53.txt

**Answer 1:**

```
abc123
01234567890
A1B2C3D4E5
6F7G8H9I0J
```

**Answer 2:**

```
456def
Hello World!
01234567890
6F7G8H9I0J
Quoth the raven: 'Nevermore.'
```

**Answer 3:**

```
abc123
456def
password
01234567890
```

# Lab 53–Search Text Files Using Regular Expressions: Extended Regex

    A1B2C3D4E5
    6F7G8H9I0J

## Answer 4:

    abc123
    456def
    01234567890
    A1B2C3D4E5
    6F7G8H9I0J

## Answer 5:

    <html>
    Quoth the raven: 'Nevermore.'

## Answer 6:

   (No output)

## Answer 7:

    Hello World!
    password

## Answer 8:

    abc123
    456def
    <html>
    _ello _orld!
    password
    01234567890
    _1_2_3_4_5
    6_7_8_9_0_
    _uoth the raven: '_evermore.'

## Answer 9:

    abc123
    456def
    <html>
    Hello World!
    [omitted]
    01234567890
    A1B2C3D4E5
    6F7G8H9I0J
    Quoth the raven: 'Nevermore.'

**Answer 10:**

```
abc123
456def
<html>
He**o World!
pa**word
01234567890
A1B2C3D4E5
6F7G8H9I0J
Quoth the raven: 'Nevermore.'
```

**Notes:**

Regexr is a great resource for practicing your regular expressions. See `man 7 regex` for more information on regex as supported by your distro.

# LAB 54

# Basic File Editing: vi Navigation

**Lab Objective:**
Learn how to open, close, and navigate the `vi` editor.

**Lab Purpose:**
In this lab, you will learn about one of the classic (but often opaque to new users) Linux text editors, `vi`.

**Lab Tool:**
Ubuntu 18.04 (or another distro of your choice)

**Lab Topology:**
A single Linux machine, or virtual machine

**Lab Walkthrough:**

*Task 1:*
Open the Terminal and run `vi /etc/passwd`. Assuming you've not run this as root, `vi` should tell you at the bottom that the file is read-only. That's fine, since you won't be making any changes right now. Instead, explore just navigating `vi`:

- Use the h, j, k, and l keys, or the arrow keys, to navigate the cursor between characters and lines.
- Enter /username, or ?username, to search forward and backward, respectively, for your username. Use n or N to hop to the next/previous match, respectively.
- Enter 10G to hop to line 10. Then just enter G to hop to the bottom of the file.
- Finally, type :q to quit. Or if you've somehow accidentally made changes, type :q! to force quit without saving them. If you are in insert mode press Esc first and then : when the cursor appears in the bottom left you can press q!

**Notes:**
The EDITOR environment variable defines which editor is used by programs that ask for one, such as `sudoedit`. By default this may be set to `nano`. If you're comfortable enough with `vi`, you may want to change this variable.

# LAB 55

# Basic File Editing: vi Modes

**Lab Objective:**
Learn how to use modes within the `vi` editor.

**Lab Purpose:**
In this lab, you will learn about one of the classic (but often opaque to new users) Linux text editors, `vi`.

**Lab Tool:**
Ubuntu 18.04 (or another distro of your choice)

**Lab Topology:**
A single Linux machine, or virtual machine

**Lab Walkthrough:**

*Task 1:*
Open the Terminal and run `vi lab55.txt`. Now, explore the modes of `vi`:

- Type i to enter insertion mode, and enter a few lines of text. Type ESC to leave this mode.
- Navigate to the middle of a line and type a to enter insertion mode one character after the cursor's position. Enter more text or hit ESC to exit the mode.
- Navigate to the middle of a line and type I to insert text at the beginning of this line. Hit ESC to exit insertion mode.
- Type A to add text at the end of the current line. Again, hit ESC to exit.
- Navigate to a line and type o to add a line of text below it. Hit ESC to exit insertion mode.
- Type O to add a line of text above the line where your cursor is. Again, hit ESC to exit.
- Use y to copy ("yank") text; for example, y$ to yank from the cursor to the end of a line, or yy to yank the whole line. Then, press p to paste.

- Use d to delete text; for example, d$ to delete from the cursor to the end of a line, or dd to delete the whole line. Type x a few times to delete a few characters under the cursor.
- Finally, use :q! to quit, or if you've written something useful, :w! to save it. You may also use :wq!, :x, or ZZ to save and quit.

**Notes:**

Hopefully, you can see that there is symmetry among `vi` commands—a/A, o/O, y/yy and d/dd, etc. Now that you're a `vi` pro, install and try its improved version, `vim`!

# LAB 56

# Create Partitions and Filesystems

**Lab Objective:**
Learn how to configure disk partitions and filesystems.

**Lab Purpose:**
In this lab, you will learn about partitioning disks using tools such as `parted`, and creating filesystems with tools such as `mkfs`.

Note: `fdisk` was covered extensively in Lab 32, and so will not be covered here. It is recommended to do Lab 32 to learn more about `fdisk`.

**Lab Tool:**
Ubuntu 18.04 (or another distro of your choice)

**Lab Topology:**
A single Linux machine, or virtual machine

**Lab Walkthrough:**

*Task 1:*
The first step is to create a dummy block device to be used in the rest of the lab, so you don't erase any of your machine's actual data. Open a terminal and run:

```
dd if=/dev/zero of=block.img bs=100M count=10
```

This file is only 1GB in size. It doesn't need to be large, but if you have more space you can make it larger for more flexibility. Now run:

- `sudo losetup -fP block.img`
- `losetup -a | grep block.img | cut -d: -f1`

This should print a device name such as /dev/loop0. This is the loopback block device, and is what should be substituted everywhere you see [dev] for the rest of this lab.

## Task 2:

Now you will partition this new block device. `gdisk` is a useful tool for creating GPT partition tables. It is based on `fdisk` and the syntax is nearly identical, so please reference Lab 32 to learn about `gdisk`. For now, use `parted` instead:

```
sudo parted [dev]
```

You can use `parted` non-interactively, but here, run the following commands in interactive mode:

- `mklabel gpt`
- `mkpart primary ext4 0 50%`
- `mkpart primary linux-swap 50% -1s`
- `quit`

These changes may prompt some warnings; they are not important for this case and you should respond in the affirmative.

It is worth noting that, unlike `fdisk` and `gdisk`, `parted` does not store all changes in memory and write them at the end, but writes every change made as you make it. Thus, it might be considered less safe than the previous two.

## Task 3:

Now create an ext4 filesystem on the first partition of your block device. The name should end in "p1"—for example, if your block device is /dev/loop0, the first partition should be /dev/loop0p1: `sudo mkfs.ext4 [dev]p1`

Finally, create a swap partition as well: `sudo mkswap [dev]p2`

If you were actually setting up a new system, you would then activate the swap partition with `swapon`, but in this case you should not do that. You could also mount the `[dev]p1` partition, and start using it as a normal ext4 filesystem if you wanted to.

## Task 4:
Clean up:

- `sudo losetup -d [dev]`
- `rm block.img`

## Notes:
In this lab you only created an ext4 filesystem—ext4 is one of the most common filesystems used on Linux today, but it is far from the only option. Under what circumstances might you choose XFS, VFAT, exFAT, or Btrfs, instead?

# LAB 57

# Maintain the Integrity of Filesystems

**Lab Objective:**
Learn how to verify filesystem integrity and repair basic problems.

**Lab Purpose:**
In this lab, you will use tools such as fsck and xfs_repair to search for filesystem problems, as well as learn how to monitor free space and inodes.

**Lab Tool:**
Ubuntu 18.04 (or another distro of your choice)

**Lab Topology:**
A single Linux machine, or virtual machine

**Lab Walkthrough:**

*Task 1:*
First, set up a dummy block device for use in the rest of this lab:

- ```
  dd if=/dev/zero of=block.img bs=100M count=10
  ```
- ```
  sudo losetup -fP block.img
  ```
- ```
  losetup -a | grep block.img | cut -d: -f1
  ```

This should print a device name such as /dev/loop0. This is the loopback block device, and is what should be substituted everywhere you see [dev] for the rest of this lab (ignore all warnings you may see for parted).

Continue with:

- ```
  sudo parted [dev] mklabel gpt
  ```
- ```
  sudo parted [dev] mkpart primary ext4 0 50%
  ```
- ```
  sudo parted [dev] "mkpart primary xfs 50% -1s"
  ```
- ```
  sudo mkfs.ext4 [dev]p1
  ```
  ```

- sudo apt -y install xfsprogs
- sudo mkfs.xfs [dev]p2
- mkdir lab57-ext4 lab57-xfs
- sudo mount [dev]p1 lab57-ext4
- sudo mount [dev]p2 lab57-xfs
- sudo dd if=/dev/urandom of=lab57-ext4/random bs=1M count=500
- sudo dd if=/dev/urandom of=lab57-xfs/random bs=1M count=500
- md5sum lab57-{ext4,xfs}/random

What you've just done is created two filesystems on your block device and filled them up with a file containing random data. Then you obtained the md5 hash of each file, which you should save for later.

*Task 2:*
Now, you get to do something you would never do on a live system... cause damage, intentionally!

- sudo umount [dev]p1 [dev]p2
- sudo dd if=/dev/urandom bs=1 count=10M of=[dev]p1 seek=1M
- sudo dd if=/dev/urandom bs=1 count=10M of=[dev]p2 seek=1M

You've just caused some significant corruption to both filesystems, though unfortunately because of the nature of such corruption, the results can't be predicted. What you should do is attempt to remount both filesystems and get the MD5 sums again:

- sudo mount [dev]p1 lab57-ext4
- sudo mount [dev]p2 lab57-xfs
- md5sum lab57-{ext4,xfs}/random

However, it's possible that md5sum or even mount will fail for one or both filesystems. Make sure the filesystems are unmounted again, then run:

- sudo fsck [dev]p1
- sudo xfs_repair [dev]p2

You should then be able to mount the filesystems again. However, you may notice that the MD5 sums of your "important" data have been permanently altered. This is the unfortunate fact of filesystem corruption—not everything can always be saved.

## Lab 57—Maintain the Integrity of Filesystems

*Task 3:*
Check disk space on both filesystems with:

- `du -hs lab57*`
- `df -h [dev]*`

Are they still full, or where one or both of your files actually deleted because of the corruption?

*Task 4:*
Finally, clean up:

- `sudo umount lab57*`
- `sudo losetup -d [dev]`
- `rm block.img`
- `rmdir lab57*`

**Notes:**
Both ext4 and XFS have advanced tuning parameters for a variety of needs. See the man pages for `tune2fs`, `xfs_fsr`, and `xfs_db`.

# LAB 58

# Control Mounting and Unmounting of Filesystems: Manual Mounting

**Lab Objective:**
Learn how to manually mount and unmount Linux filesystems.

**Lab Purpose:**
In this lab, you will learn how to manually mount/unmount filesystems and how to identify filesystems via labels and UUID's.

**Lab Tool:**
Ubuntu 18.04 (or another distro of your choice)

**Lab Topology:**
A single Linux machine, or virtual machine

**Lab Walkthrough:**

*Task 1:*
Open the Terminal and run:

- `lsblk -f`
- `blkid`

These are two commands which can get you information on your block device labels and UUID's. By default your root filesystem and other filesystems may not have labels—if they do, `lsblk -f` will print those labels, which can then be passed to `blkid`.

*Task 2:*
Now run `mount` to identify what filesystems are currently mounted. If you have an external USB drive, you could insert that, use `lsblk -f` to identify it, and then mount/unmount it with `mount` and `umount`.

**Notes:**
For information about default filesystems, see the /etc/fstab file and `man fstab`.

# LAB 59

# Control Mounting and Unmounting of Filesystems: Automatic Mounting

**Lab Objective:**
Learn how to automatically mount Linux filesystems.

**Lab Purpose:**
In this lab, you will learn how to automatically mount a filesystem on a Linux system at boot, using the /etc/fstab file.

**Lab Tool:**
Ubuntu 18.04 (or another distro of your choice)

**Lab Topology:**
A single Linux machine, or virtual machine

**Lab Walkthrough:**

*Task 1:*
First, you will need another filesystem to mount. This can be an external disk, or a loopback block device that you create for this purpose (see Lab 56). Identify the label or UUID of this device, then open /etc/fstab with your favorite editor. One way to identify the UUID is with `sudo lsblk -f`.

Add a line for this new device. The details will vary based on the device, but here is a template:

```
UUID=01234567-89ab-cdef-0123-456789abcdef /mnt/mydevice vfat defaults 0 2
```

The UUID for my CDROM drive (sr0) is listed below:

```
sda
└─sda1  ext4                         39584296-303a-4700-a8cd-8386f2f792cb /
sr0     iso9660  VBox_GAs_5.2.18 2018-08-14-11-58-42-18                   /
media/paul/VBox_GAs_5.2.1
```

I then applied the below line to /etc/fstab:

```
UUID=2018-08-14-11-58-42-18 /media iso9660 defaults 0 2
```

When in doubt, check the man pages: `man fstab`

Save and close the file, reboot your machine, and check mounted filesystems with `mount`. If you did everything correctly, your device should be mounted!

**Notes:**

Users with experience in networked filesystems such as NFS may want to read about `autofs`, a tool to automatically mount filesystems as they are needed.

# LAB 60

# Manage File Permissions and Ownership: File Permissions

**Lab Objective:**
Learn how to manipulate permissions and ownership settings of files.

**Lab Purpose:**
In this lab, you will learn to use `chmod`, `chown`, and `chgrp`, as well as `umask`.

**Lab Tool:**
Ubuntu 18.04 (or another distro of your choice)

**Lab Topology:**
A single Linux machine, or virtual machine

**Lab Walkthrough:**

*Task 1:*
Open the Terminal and run:

- `echo "Hello World" > foo`
- `ls -l foo`

Look at the first field; you should see `-rw-r--r--`

This indicates the user, group, and other permissions. The last nine characters, in groups of three, denote these permissions. In this instance:

- `rw-` indicates read/write (but not execute) permissions for the user who owns the file
- `r--` indicates read-only permissions for the group that owns the file
- `r--` indicates read-only permissions for all non-owners, a.k.a. "world"

The first character indicates the type of file. In this case it is a regular file; directories begin with `d`.

Who are the user and group owners of this file? The third and fourth fields of `ls -l` tell us that. By default, it should be your own user and primary group.

*Task 2:*
Now run:

- `sudo chown root foo`
- `ls -l foo`
- `cat foo`

You've just changed the user ownership to root, while keeping the group ownership. As the file has group- and world-read permissions, you can still see its contents.

*Task 3:*
Now run:

- `sudo chmod o-r foo`
- `ls -l foo`
- `cat foo`

That `chmod` command removes read permissions from foo. However, as you still have group ownership, you can still see the file's contents.

*Task 4:*
Now run:

- `sudo chgrp root foo`
- `sudo chmod 600 foo`
- `ls -l foo`
- `cat foo`

This `chmod` command sets the permissions explicitly, to read-write for the owning user only. As that is root, we can no longer read the file.

*Task 5:*
The default permissions for a newly created file can be adjusted with `umask`. This serves to "mask out," at a bit level, permissions that a new file should not have. Run the following

- `u=$(umask)`
- `umask 0777`

## Lab 60–Manage File Permissions and Ownership: File Permissions

- `touch bar`
- `ls -l bar`
- `umask $u`

The bar file should have no permissions set—you've masked them all out with `umask`.

### Task 6:
Finally, clean up with `sudo rm foo bar`

**Notes:**
The first octal bit of `chmod` deals with setuid and setgid (and the sticky bit, on directories). When set, these bits will run an executable file as the user/group owner, rather than the user running the executable. This opens up security risks, particularly when a program is owned by root. For this reason, most systems will ignore the setuid/setgid bits when set on shell scripts.

# LAB 61

# Manage File Permissions and Ownership: Directory Permissions

**Lab Objective:**
Learn how to manipulate permissions and ownership settings of directories.

**Lab Purpose:**
In this lab, you will learn to use `chmod`, `chown`, and `chgrp`, as well as `umask`, and their implications for directories.

**Lab Tool:**
Ubuntu 18.04 (or another distro of your choice)

**Lab Topology:**
A single Linux machine, or virtual machine

**Lab Walkthrough:**

*Task 1:*
Open the Terminal and run:

- `mkdir foo`
- `echo "Hello World" > foo/bar`
- `ls -la foo`

Look at the first field; you should see `drwxr-xr-x`

This indicates the user, group, and other permissions. The first 'd' just indicates a directory. The last nine characters, in groups of three, denote these permissions. In this instance:

- `rwx` indicates read/write/execute permissions for the user who owns the file
- `r-x` indicates read/execute permissions for the group that owns the file
- `r-x` indicates read/execute permissions for all non-owners, a.k.a. "world"

Who are the user and group owners of this file? The third and fourth fields of `ls -l` tell us that. By default, it should be your own user and primary group.

## Task 2:
Now run:

- `sudo chown root foo`
- `ls -la foo`
- `cat foo/bar`

You've just changed the user ownership to root, while keeping the group ownership. As the directory has group- and world-read permissions, you can still see its contents.

## Task 3:
Now run:

- `sudo chmod o-r foo`
- `ls -la foo`
- `cat foo/bar`

That `chmod` command removes read permissions from foo. However, as you still have group ownership, you can still see the file's contents.

## Task 4:
Now run:

- `sudo chgrp root foo`
- `ls -la foo`
- `ls -ld foo`
- `cat foo/bar`

You've now set yourself up with execute-only permissions on the foo directory, which is an interesting scenario. You no longer have permissions to view the contents of the directory, nor to add new files to it... but if you already know that a given file exists, your permissions for that file still allow you to act on it. In this example, you can view the contents of foo/bar, and even still modify them! This also applies to any subdirectories under foo.

## Task 5:
Now run:

- `sudo chmod 2777 foo`
- `touch foo/baz`
- `ls -l foo/baz`

## Lab 61–Manage File Permissions and Ownership: Directory Permissions

What you did was set the setgid bit for this directory, which causes files created under it to have the same group ownership as the directory itself. In practice, this is a way to ensure a group of users sharing files doesn't have to worry as much about permissions.

### Task 6:
The default permissions for a newly created file can be adjusted with `umask`. This serves to "mask out," at a bit level, permissions that a new file should not have. Run the following

- `u=$(umask)`
- `umask 0777`
- `mkdir bar`
- `ls -ld bar`
- `umask $u`

The bar directory should have no permissions set—you've masked them all out with `umask`.

### Task 6:
Finally, clean up with `sudo rm -r foo bar`

### Notes:
Another special bit specific to directories is called the sticky bit, which is covered in Lab 25. This bit, set on a world-writable directory, ensures that users can only remove or modify files that they themselves own. This is most useful on /tmp.

# LAB 62

# Create and Change Hard and Symbolic Links

**Lab Objective:**
Learn how to create and manage hard links and symbolic links.

**Lab Purpose:**
In this lab, you will work with hard links, symbolic (soft) links, and learn the difference between copying and linking.

**Lab Tool:**
Ubuntu 18.04 (or another distro of your choice)

**Lab Topology:**
A single Linux machine, or virtual machine

**Lab Walkthrough:**

*Task 1:*

Open the Terminal and run:

- `touch foo`
- `ln -sv foo myfoo`
- `ls -l myfoo`
- `echo hello > foo`
- `cat myfoo`
- `rm myfoo`
- `ls -l foo`

What just happened? You created a *symbolic link* to a file (foo) called myfoo. The `ls` output shows this link. A symbolic link is simply a reference to an existing file. This way, you may have multiple references to a single file—edit the original file, and all of the references instantly update, as shown by `cat`.

When you remove the link, the original file still remains. (If you remove the original file while keeping the symlink, you will have what's called a *broken link*, just like on the internet.) This is useful for some system configurations.

*Task 2:*
Now run:

- `ln -v foo myfoo`
- `echo goodbye > foo`
- `cat myfoo`
- `rm foo`
- `ls -l myfoo`
- `cat myfoo`

You just created a different type of link, called a *hard link*. Hard links behave similarly to symlinks in the sense that when the original is modified the links follow, and vice versa. However, a hard link keeps its data if the original file is deleted. Hard links also cannot be made across filesystem or partition boundaries, and directories cannot be hard-linked.

*Task 3:*
Finally, clean up with `rm myfoo`

**Notes:**
Under the hood, hard links are really acting upon *inodes*. A hard link creates another file pointing to the same inode as the original file. (Symlinks work at a higher level, pointing directly to a file or directory name.) You can see the inode number with `ls -i`, or see how many hard links share a given file's inode in the second column of `ls -l`

# LAB 63

## Find System Files and Place Files in the Correct Location

**Lab Objective:**
Learn how to locate files on a Linux system.

**Lab Purpose:**
In this lab, you will learn multiple ways of locating files on a system, in accordance with the Filesystem Hierarchy Standard (FHS).

**Lab Tool:**
Ubuntu 18.04 (or another distro of your choice)

**Lab Topology:**
A single Linux machine, or virtual machine

**Lab Walkthrough:**

*Task 1:*
In previous labs, you've worked with `find`, a tool which can find files fitting a certain specification and even execute commands on those files. `find` is great for a limited scope, but becomes unwieldy when you don't actually know where a given file is located, because then it has to search the entire filesystem! There's another way. Open the Terminal and run:

- `sudo updatedb`
- `locate updatedb.conf`

As you might guess, `locate` operates from a database which is updated by `updatedb`. The `updatedb` command may take a couple of minutes, but once it's done, every subsequent `locate` will be very fast.

Here, you should have found two files: One is the actual `updatedb` config file, and the other is the man page. You can investigate these now if you like:

- `cat /etc/updatedb.conf`

- `man 5 updatedb.conf`

The updatedb.conf file should include a directive to prune paths like /tmp and /media, among others. Given what you know about the FHS: Why do you think it's a good idea to prune these paths from the `locate` database? Why is it a good idea to prune filesystem types like nfs and proc?

*Task 2:*
Now run:

- `which which`
- `which locate`
- `whereis locate`
- `whereis updatedb`
- `whereis whereis`

`which` shows you the absolute location of a given (relative) command, while `whereis` expands on this by showing other related files like config files, databases, and man pages.

**Notes:**
Many common Linux tools are fairly complicated C programs; `which` is one exception. It is a short shell script which, with a bit of practice, you could understand in its entirety. Take a look at the /bin/which file and see how much of it makes sense to you!

# LPIC1 Linux Administrator– Exam 102

# LAB 64

## Customize and Use the Shell Environment: User Profiles

**Lab Objective:**
Learn about global and user profiles.

**Lab Purpose:**
In this lab, you will manage shell profiles and learn which files can be used to customize both global profiles and those for specific users.

**Lab Tool:**
Ubuntu 18.04 (or another distro of your choice)

**Lab Topology:**
A single Linux machine, or virtual machine

**Lab Walkthrough:**

*Task 1:*

Open your favorite editor via the terminal, and take a look at the following files (some of these files may not exist, that's normal):

- /etc/profile
- /etc/skel/.bash_profile and/or ~/.bash_profile
- /etc/skel/.bash_login and/or ~/.bash_login
- /etc/skel/.profile and/or ~/.profile
- /etc/bash.bashrc
- /etc/skel/.bashrc and/or ~/.bashrc
- /etc/skel/.bash_logout and/or ~/.bash_logout

Bash attempts to read the first four files (in preference order) every time you start a *login* shell, while it reads the latter two whenever you start an *interactive* shell. Typically, a login shell is started once per boot, or once per SSH login, while an interactive shell is started every time you open the Terminal application (or a new tab within it)—but, as with all things, there are exceptions. Finally, Bash reads ~/.bash_logout when a login shell is exited.

You won't necessarily understand everything that's happening in these files right away. The key takeaway is that this is where you can make permanent changes to every aspect of a shell's profile, including environment variables, shell options, and even text and background colors.

*Task 2:*

Test this theory by adding a simple welcome message. Open ~/.bashrc in your favorite editor and add the following line at the end of the file:

```
echo "Welcome, $USER! You've successfully modified the .bashrc file!"
```

Save and quit, exit the terminal, then open a new terminal, and you should be greeted with your message.

Note that this only applies to your user. If you wanted it to apply to a different user, you would have to modify that user's own .bashrc file. To apply it to all future users, you would edit /etc/skel/.bashrc, or /etc/bash.bashrc to apply it to all *current* (and future) users.

**Notes:**

An interesting environment variable to experiment with is PS1. Running `echo $PS1` will print out a confusing mess of special symbols, but simply running `PS1="$ "` will make it immediately apparent that this, in fact, what defines your prompt!

# LAB 65

# Customize and Use the Shell Environment: Aliases and Functions

**Lab Objective:**
Learn about aliases and functions in Bash.

**Lab Purpose:**
In this lab, you will use aliases and functions within Bash to define "shortcuts" which may make your life easier.

**Lab Tool:**
Ubuntu 18.04 (or another distro of your choice)

**Lab Topology:**
A single Linux machine, or virtual machine

**Lab Walkthrough:**

*Task 1:*
Open the Terminal and run:

- `alias mkhello='t=$(mktemp); echo "Hello World" > $t; echo $t; unset t'`
- `mkhello`

You just created an alias that you may wish you'd had in earlier labs. This new `mkhello` command just creates a temporary file with our favorite text in it, then prints the filename for your use.

You likely already have some aliases defined for you—take a look at `grep alias ~/.bashrc`

## Task 2:

Typically you would use `alias` for simpler shortcuts (arguably, `mkhello` is even a bit too complicated). But what if you need something more complex? Now run:

- `function newdir { mkdir $1; pushd $1; ls -al; }`
- `newdir foo`
- `newdir bar`
- `newdir ~/baz`

This creates the `newdir` command by adding a bit of sugar to `mkdir`. Functions, unlike aliases, can directly use arguments. There's also another, more C-like way you could have written this:

```
newdir() { mkdir $1; pushd $1; ls -al; }
```

## Task 3:

Finally, clean up: `cd ~; rm -r foo baz`

## Notes:

One more shell trick is `source`, or `.` (the dot, which in Bash is a synonym for `source`). You don't typically use this interactively, but from a script or shell initiation file to read commands from another file. The main difference is that `source` reads these commands into the *current* shell rather than launching a new one, which is why it is not typically used on independent scripts.

# LAB 66

## Customize or Write Simple Scripts: Standard Syntax

**Lab Objective:**
Learn about standard shell syntax specific to scripting setup.

**Lab Purpose:**
In this lab, you will learn about standard shell scripting syntax, such as tests and control flow.

**Lab Tool:**
Ubuntu 18.04 (or another distro of your choice)

**Lab Topology:**
A single Linux machine, or virtual machine

**Lab Walkthrough:**

*Task 1:*
Open your favorite editor via the terminal and create a file called lab66.sh:

```sh
#!/bin/sh

i=0
while test $i -lt 5
do
  echo $i
  i=$(($i+1))
done

for file in $(ls /etc)
do
  test -r /etc/$file && echo "$file is readable by $USER."
  test -s /etc/$file || echo "$file has size zero!"
  if test -d /etc/$file
  then
    echo "$file is a directory."
  fi
done
```

This highly contrived and not very useful script contains a number of important features. The first is `test`, which can test a wide variety of conditions depending on its flags and return a 0 or 1 (true or false) exit status. That exit status can, in turn, be used by control flow syntax—`if` statements, or `for` or `while` loops. A simpler kind of `if` statement is the `&&` or `||` syntax, a boolean 'and' or 'or', respectively.

If you wish, you can test the script by executing it with:

- `chmod +x lab66.sh`
- `./lab66.sh`

You should see the numbers 0-4 printed out, followed by a large amount of text output, depending on what's in your /etc directory.

**Notes:**
This is a somewhat-rare situation where using /bin/sh and /bin/bash as the interpreter may yield different results. Bash has a `((++var))` syntax for variable incrementation, which is non-standard in the normal Bourne shell. Similar for `[[ ]]` (a test syntax) and the C-style for loop syntax: `for ((i=0; i<5; i++))`...

# LAB 67

## Customize or Write Simple Scripts: Miscellaneous Tools

**Lab Objective:**
Learn about more useful scripting commands, such as `read`, `seq`, and `exec`.

**Lab Purpose:**
In this lab, you will learn how to read input to a script with `read`, print a sequence of numbers with `seq`, and replace the current shell with `exec`.

**Lab Tool:**
Ubuntu 18.04 (or another distro of your choice)

**Lab Topology:**
A single Linux machine, or virtual machine

**Lab Walkthrough:**

*Task 1:*
Open the Terminal and run:

- `read -p "What is your name? " name`
- `<type your name>`
- `echo $name`

This is a simple use of `read`, but it can also be used to read from file descriptors rather than standard input. See the man page for more info.

*Task 2:*
`seq` is another command that's fairly straightforward to understand. Run the following:

- `seq 5`
- `seq 3 5`
- `seq 0 2 5`
- `seq 0 0.5 5`

You should see the numbers 1-5, 3-5, 0-4 (by 2), and 0-5 (by 0.5).

*Task 3:*
`exec` is a bit more complicated than the previous two. It has different behaviors depending on whether arguments are passed to it.

If arguments are passed, it executes them as a command (as if the 'exec' wasn't there) but replaces the current shell with the new command. In practice, this means any commands in a shell script which come after the `exec` will never be executed (unless `exec` is run in a subshell).

Open a new terminal and run `exec ls`—you will never see the output because the terminal will exit first!

If instead of arguments, `exec` precedes a redirect, then that redirect will apply to the rest of the script/shell. For example, if you open a new terminal and run:

- `exec > exec.log`
- `echo "Where is my echo?"`
- `ls nonexistent`

You won't see anything printed from the `echo` statement until you open exec.log, but you will see an error message from `ls`. If you run `exec &> exec.log`, all output and errors will be sent to the log file.

**Notes:**
`exec` is commonly used in wrapper scripts. These are scripts which may modify arguments or simplify the running of another program. When used this way, the wrapper script does its processing and then calls the main program with `exec`, meaning it "gets out of the way." Without `exec`, the wrapper would remain running, taking up resources and potentially confusing a user who wanted to terminate the process.

# LAB 68

## Customize or Write Simple Scripts: Scripting Practice

**Lab Objective:**
Use what you already know to write a simple shell script, from scratch.

**Lab Purpose:**
Scripting with Bash is a daily task by many professional Linux administrators. When a task is repetitive, you don't want to be typing the same list of commands over and over; you want to create a script, and perhaps also schedule that script to run automatically.

**Lab Tool:**
Ubuntu 18.04 (or another distro of your choice)

**Lab Topology:**
A single Linux machine, or virtual machine

**Lab Walkthrough:**

*Task 1:*
Open the Terminal application and run your favorite text editor.

You may wish to reference Labs 66 and 67 if you have not already done so. Your goal is to write a script which accepts three arguments—a directory path, and two flags to be passed to `test`. This script should check every file in the directory (non-recursively) and, if it passes *both* tests, prints that file's name.

Example:
```
./foo.sh ~/mydir -f -w
myfile
```

In this example, the script is looking for files with ~/mydir that are regular files with write permissions granted. myfile passes those tests.

All error conditions should print a friendly message and exit with status 1. For example, if three arguments are not passed, or the passed directory doesn't exist, or one of the `test` arguments is not valid. See **Answer 1** below for one possible solution.

For an extra challenge, you might print all files, but sort them according to how many tests they passed.

**Answer 1:**

```
#!/bin/bash

test $# -eq 3 || { echo "Exactly three arguments are required."; exit 1; }
test -d $1 || { echo "Not a directory."; exit 1; }
files=$(ls $1 2>/dev/null) || { echo "I can't read that directory."; exit 1; }

for f in $files; do
  test $2 $1/$f 2>/dev/null
  rc1=$?
  test $3 $1/$f 2>/dev/null
  rc2=$?
  test $rc1 -gt 1 && { echo "First test argument is invalid."; exit 1; }
  test $rc2 -gt 1 && { echo "Second test argument is invalid."; exit 1; }
  test $rc1 -eq 0 && test $rc2 -eq 0 && echo $f
done
```

**Notes:**

Remember that using /bin/sh as an interpreter can have different results from /bin/bash! It is good to understand what makes a *Bourne-compatible* shell, and what non-Bourne-compatible additions are available in Bash.

# LAB 69

# Install and Configure X11

**Lab Objective:**
Learn about the X11 window system and how to configure it.

**Lab Purpose:**
In this lab, you will explore various aspects of X11 configuration.

**Lab Tool:**
Ubuntu 18.04 (or another distro of your choice), and a running X11 system. If you aren't sure whether your system runs X11, test with `sudo ps -ef | egrep -i x11\|xorg`

**Lab Topology:**
A single Linux machine, or virtual machine

**Lab Walkthrough:**

*Task 1:*
Open the Terminal and attempt to look at /etc/X11/xorg.conf or /etc/X11/xorg.conf.d. These paths may not exist—on a default Ubuntu 18.04 VM install, they don't. If not, run blah and take a look there instead—for example, in /usr/share/X11/xorg.conf.d. You are just trying to view some example Xorg config files.

A typical X11 config will have one or more sections, each section dealing with a single device; for example, a monitor, or a graphics card, or an input device. Within a section, a given device may have several directives, like specifying a driver or various options for the device.

If you are setting up Xorg on a new server, you can run `Xorg -configure` to generate a new configuration. This is not recommended on a machine of any importance, as it is easy to mess up. (Though a backup should be automatically created.)

*Task 2:*
Now run:

- `echo $DISPLAY`
- `xhost`
- `xauth list`

These commands will print your Xorg display number, authorized hosts, and authorization entries, respectively. In nearly all cases, the first output should be `:0`, and the second output should be something like `SI:localuser:ubuntu`. The only situation in which this would be radically different is if your machine was used as a remote X server, and especially if you were connected to X remotely. (In practice, this is rare—most Linux professionals manage remote servers via SSH only.) The third output lists authorization entries, or "magic cookies", for each display.

**Notes:**
Wayland is a newer windowing system that aims to replace X11. Ubuntu used Wayland as default in version 17.10, but moved back to X11 in 18.04 due to bugs. It is worth understanding both Wayland and X11.

# LAB 70

# Graphical Desktops

**Lab Objective:**
Learn about different Linux display managers and desktop environments.

**Lab Purpose:**
In this lab, you will learn about Linux desktop environments by installing and using another one on your lab machine.

**Lab Tool:**
Ubuntu 18.04 (or another distro of your choice)

**Lab Topology:**
A single Linux machine, or virtual machine

**Lab Walkthrough:**

*Task 1:*
In this lab, your challenge is to select, install, and use a desktop environment which you have not used before. On a default Ubuntu system, GNOME and GDM are in use, so don't select that one. XFCE4 is recommended, but there are other options. To install it on your current system: `sudo apt install xfce4`

This will take a while, after which you should log out. Upon doing so, you should be prompted to select a display manager and log back in.

If you do not see a new option and don't know how to fix it, or just don't want to risk messing up your lab machine, there is an alternative: Install **Xubuntu** on another virtual machine. Xubuntu is an Ubuntu derivative that comes with XFCE pre-installed and configured.

**Notes:**
This article contains a decent, if not 100% complete, round-up of desktop environments you might like to consider.

https://www.makeuseof.com/tag/linux-desktop-environment-best-personality/

# LAB 71

# Accessibility

**Lab Objective:**
Learn how to configure accessibility features within Linux.

**Lab Purpose:**
In this lab, you will examine various accessibility settings on a Linux desktop.

**Lab Tool:**
Ubuntu 18.04 (or another distro of your choice)

**Lab Topology:**
A single Linux machine, or virtual machine

**Lab Walkthrough:**

*Task 1:*
Open the Settings application, then click Universal Access in the left sidebar.

Experiment with the following settings:

- High Contrast
- Large Text
- Cursor Size
- Zoom
- Screen Reader
- Screen Keyboard
- Repeat Keys
- Mouse Keys (see the menu in the upper right after selecting this option)

**Notes:**
Some accessibility features require specific hardware. For example, gestures are obviously more meaningful on a touch-screen device or with an external drawing tablet.

# LAB 72

# Manage User and Group Accounts and Related System Files: Users

**Lab Objective:**
Learn how to add, modify, and remove users.

**Lab Purpose:**
In this lab, you will learn about the different types of Linux users and a few tools to add, modify, and remove them.

**Lab Tool:**
Ubuntu 18.04 (or another distro of your choice)

**Lab Topology:**
A single Linux machine, or virtual machine

**Lab Walkthrough:**

*Task 1:*
Open the Terminal and run: `cat /etc/passwd`

This file is an inventory of all users on your system. The passwd file is a database with seven fields, separated by colons:

- Username
- Encrypted password (in practice, hardly ever used—see below)
- User ID
- Group ID
- Comment
- Home directory
- Default shell

Take note of the *root* user, which should be listed on the first line. This is the administrative user, and is the only user that can unconditionally do anything on the system. By running a command preceded with `sudo`, you are running that command as the root user. (You can also use `sudo -i` or `su` to access a root shell directly.)

If you look at the user ID's, you will notice that most of them, on a default system, are below 1000. These are *system* users, typically used to run specific services, rather than running those as root, which can create security problems. On most systems, human user ID's begin at 1000 or 500.

You can easily see the passwd information for your own user with: `grep ^$USER /etc/passwd`

## Task 2:
Now run: `sudo cat /etc/shadow`

The shadow file is a sensitive database containing hashed user passwords, among other information. Be careful with the contents of this file! It contains nine fields, again, separated by colons—however, on a default Ubuntu install, only the first three are likely to be significant:

1. Username
2. Encrypted password
3. Date of last password change

The other fields contain information like account expiration dates and minimum/maximum password ages, which are not configured on a default system. See `man 5 shadow` for more information.

You can see this information for your own user with: `sudo grep ^$USER /etc/shadow`

## Task 3:
Now run:

```
sudo sh -c 'echo "Hello World" > /etc/skel/hello.txt'
```

Here, you are adding a file to the /etc/skel directory, which determines the default files in a new user's home directory.

Now:

- `sudo useradd -m foo`
- `sudo cat ~foo/hello.txt`

## LAB 72–MANAGE USER AND GROUP ACCOUNTS AND RELATED SYSTEM FILES: USERS

You should see the output "Hello World". What happened is that you created a new user, called foo (using the `-m` switch to ensure a home directory was created). Every file in /etc/skel was then copied to the new user's home directory.

Finally, set an initial password for this user with: `sudo passwd foo`

*Task 4:*
Finally, clean up:

- `sudo rm /etc/skel/hello.txt`
- `sudo userdel foo`
- `sudo rm -r /home/foo`

**Notes:**
`usermod` is a very useful command for managing users. In addition to adding and removing users from groups, it allows you to manage account/password expirations and other security features. `usermod` will be discussed in the next two labs.

# LAB 73

# Manage User and Group Accounts and Related System Files: Groups

**Lab Objective:**
Learn how to add, modify, and remove groups.

**Lab Purpose:**
In this lab, you will learn about Linux groups and a few tools to add, modify, and remove them.

**Lab Tool:**
Ubuntu 18.04 (or another distro of your choice)

**Lab Topology:**
A single Linux machine, or virtual machine

**Lab Walkthrough:**

*Task 1:*
Open the Terminal and run: `cat /etc/group`

As you might expect, this is a database of all groups on the system. It contains four fields separated by colons:

- Group name
- Encrypted group password
- Group ID
- List of users who are members

Run `groups` to learn which groups your user has membership in. You can get more information, including group ID's, with the `id` command.

## Task 2:
Now let's create a group and add ourselves to it:

- `sudo groupadd foo`
- `sudo usermod -a -G foo $USER`

Verify that your user was added with: `grep ^foo /etc/group`

## Task 3:
You can use groupmod to change properties of the group, like its name:

- `sudo groupmod -n bar foo`
- `grep ^bar /etc/group`

Finally, clean up with `sudo groupdel bar`

**Notes:**
Several directives in /etc/login.defs will affect the behavior of `groupadd` and `groupmod`. See the man pages for `groupadd`, `groupmod`, and login.defs for more information.

# LAB 74

# Manage User and Group Accounts and Related System Files: Special Purpose Accounts

**Lab Objective:**
Learn how to manage special-purpose user accounts.

**Lab Purpose:**
In this lab, you will learn about the special purpose and limited user accounts, and how to create and manage them.

**Lab Tool:**
Ubuntu 18.04 (or another distro of your choice)

**Lab Topology:**
A single Linux machine, or virtual machine

**Lab Walkthrough:**

*Task 1:*
Open the Terminal and add a system user: `sudo useradd -r foo`

When adding a system user, `useradd` does not any account or password aging information, and sets a user ID appropriate for a system user (typically below 1000). It also does not create a home directory unless you specify `-m`.

`getent` is a cleaner way of getting entries from passwd, group, and other administrative databases. Inspect the new user with: `sudo getent passwd foo`

`getent --help` will tell you which databases are supported.

## Task 2:
Now add another user account which we will apply some limitations to:

```
sudo useradd -s /usr/sbin/nologin bar
```

You've created an account with a special shell that is... well, not a shell at all. It just displays a message that the account is not available. (Test this with `sudo su bar`) You might use this in combination with the `-r` flag to create a non-interactive system user, solely for the purpose of running daemons or other specific processes.

## Task 3:
Now run:

- `sudo usermod -s /bin/bash bar`
- `sudo passwd bar`
- `<give the user a password>`
- `sudo chage -E 1 bar`
- `su bar`

Here, you've switched to a valid shell and changed the password for user bar, but then you used `chage` (*ch*ange *age*) to set the account as expired, so you once again cannot log in.

Sometimes you may want to lock a user's password but not the account itself (preserving access for root, or for SSH keys, for example). You would do this with `sudo usermod -L bar`

## Task 4:
Finally, clean up:

- `sudo userdel foo`
- `sudo userdel bar`

**Notes:**
It is recommended to look over the /etc/login.defs file for a complete understanding of limitations and privileges that can be applied to Linux accounts.

# LAB 75

# Automate System Administration Tasks by Scheduling Jobs: Cron

**Lab Objective:**
Learn how to use cron utilities to schedule automated system tasks.

**Lab Purpose:**
In this lab, you will manage automated system tasks using the classic `cron` utilities.

**Lab Tool:**
Ubuntu 18.04 (or another distro of your choice)

**Lab Topology:**
A single Linux machine, or virtual machine

**Lab Walkthrough:**

*Task 1:*
Open the Terminal and run: `cat /etc/crontab`

In this file, you will likely see a few rows of commands to be run at certain times. The first five columns designate the minute, hour, day-of-month, month, and day-of-year, respectively, for a given job to be run. Then you will see the user (usually root) and, finally, the actual command. See `man 5 crontab` for a full description of crontab format.

On a default Ubuntu installation, /etc/crontab should contain "meta" commands to run cron jobs from other files—/etc/cron.hourly, /etc/cron.daily, and so forth. Look at these next:

```
ls /etc/cron.{hourly,daily,weekly,monthly,d}
```

As you might guess, these directories hold jobs to be run hourly, daily, weekly, monthly, or on some other interval. Inspect a few files to see what jobs are run periodically on your system.

On some systems, a user-based crontab is used. In this case, run `crontab -l` and `sudo crontab -l` to view the jobs. These jobs are stored in /var/spool/cron/crontabs.

*Task 2:*
Run `crontab -e` and add a cron job for your user:

```
* * * * * date > ~/foo
```

Then: `sleep 60 && cat ~/foo`

You should see that your cron job has run (every minute) and printed the date into file foo. Clean up with `crontab -e`, delete the line you added, and `rm foo`

**Notes:**
/etc/cron.allow and /etc/cron.deny control user access to `crontab`. On a default Ubuntu system, these files may not exist—according to the man page, that means only root should have access to `crontab`, but default system configuration allows *all* users access. See `man crontab` to understand how these files work.

# LAB 76

# Automate System Administration Tasks by Scheduling Jobs: At and Systemd

**Lab Objective:**
Learn how to use `at` and Systemd utilities to schedule automated system tasks.

**Lab Purpose:**
In this lab, you will manage automated system tasks with Systemd and scheduled tasks using `at`.

**Lab Tool:**
Ubuntu 18.04 (or another distro of your choice)

**Lab Topology:**
A single Linux machine, or virtual machine

**Lab Walkthrough:**

*Task 1:*
Open the Terminal and run: `sudo apt install at`

In contrast to `cron`, `at` is used for running one-time jobs at some time in the future.

Now run:

- `echo "touch foo" | at now + 1 min`
- `atq`
- `sleep 60 && ls foo`
- `rm foo`

You scheduled a `touch foo` command to be run in the future; `atq` shows this job (which you could delete if you wanted to, using `atrm`). One small caveat, though—`at` will not necessarily schedule your job *exactly* one minute in the future, when used with this syntax. The seconds are truncated, so, in fact, it may run less than one second from "now". `at` isn't generally used in scenarios requiring such precision!

Like with cron, `at` can be user-restricted in the /etc/at.allow and /etc/at.deny files. In Ubuntu, by default, a blacklist is set up—see this with `cat /etc/at.deny`

*Task 2:*
Any Systemd service can be configured with a timer, which can use an OnCalendar directive to mimic `cron`, for example:

```
...
[Timer]
OnCalendar=*-*-* 03:30:00
Persistent=true
...
```

See `man systemd.timer` for more info.

You can also create transient timer units, a la `at`, with `systemd-run`:

```
systemd-run --on-active=60 touch ~/foo
```

That will touch a file after 60 seconds. This can also be used with pre-existing services, for example, if you have a unit called *myunit:*

```
systemd-run --on-active="12h" --unit myunit.service
```

**Notes:**
Though Systemd can effectively replace both `cron` and `at`, it is not without problems. Cron-like jobs especially take far more time to set up within Systemd, compared to adding a single line to a crontab file.

# LAB 77

## Localization and Internationalization: Timezones

**Lab Objective:**
Learn how to configure timezone settings.

**Lab Purpose:**
In this lab, you will learn how timezones work in Linux and how to configure their settings.

**Lab Tool:**
Ubuntu 18.04 (or another distro of your choice)

**Lab Topology:**
A single Linux machine, or virtual machine

**Lab Walkthrough:**

*Task 1:*
Open the Terminal and run:

- `cat /etc/timezone`
- `ls -l /etc/localtime`
- `file /usr/share/zoneinfo/$(< /etc/timezone)`

These commands just print a bit of information about your configured local timezone. /etc/timezone contains a designator, while /etc/localtime should be a symlink to a file under /usr/share/zoneinfo. As the third command shows, this is not a human-readable file, but `file` can still share some information about it.

*Task 2:*
Now run: `tzselect`

Going through this interactive process will, at the end, print out your timezone (which is hopefully already configured) and note how you can make it permanent for your user by setting the TZ environment variable.

Finally, use `timedatectl` to print out some additional information, and `date` to get the current time. Both commands have several more options described by their man pages.

**Notes:**

If your lab machine is a VM running on hardware that is often put into sleep or hibernation, you may find that your VM's RTC time has drifted. To fix this, you can enable NTP in the VM:

```
systemctl enable --now systemd-timesyncd
```

# LAB 78

## Localisation and Internationalisation: Locales

**Lab Objective:**
Learn how to configure locale settings.

**Lab Purpose:**
In this lab, you will learn how locales work in Linux and how to configure their settings and environment variables.

**Lab Tool:**
Ubuntu 18.04 (or another distro of your choice)

**Lab Topology:**
A single Linux machine, or virtual machine

**Lab Walkthrough:**

*Task 1:*
Open the Terminal and run: `locale`

You should see a number of variables, the first of which being LANG—as you might guess, this is the locale setting for your default language. Several other variables are listed below it, naming the settings for dates/times, phone numbers, currency, and other designations.

To see the locale settings currently supported by your system: `locale -a`

And to see supported character maps: `locale -m`

Your default locale settings are probably some variation of UTF-8, which is a standard character map on Linux.

**LPIC1 LINUX ADMINISTRATOR–EXAM 102**

*Task 2:*

If you're feeling daring (this is not recommended), you can use update-locale to change your settings to a radically different language and/or character map. For example, `sudo update-locale LANG=<setting>`

LANG=C is notable for being useful in scripting -- it disables localization and uses the default language so that output is consistent.

**Notes:**

You can use `iconv` to convert text between character encodings.

# LAB 79

# Maintain System Time: NTP

**Lab Objective:**
Learn how to maintain system time and synchronize the clock with NTP.

**Lab Purpose:**
In this lab, you will learn about the classic Network Time Protocol (NTP) and its settings for synchronizing the system clock.

**Lab Tool:**
Ubuntu 18.04 (or another distro of your choice)

**Lab Topology:**
A single Linux machine, or virtual machine

**Lab Walkthrough:**

*Task 1:*
Open the Terminal and run: `sudo apt install ntp ntpdate`

Now view the main NTP configuration file with: `cat /etc/ntp.conf`

NTP works by synchronizing time in a tree topology—your lab machine gets its time from a distro-specific pool of servers, specified by "pool" (for example, *.ubuntu.pool.ntp.org). Ubuntu's own servers get their times from some upstream source, and so on, all the way up to a system of atomic clocks in laboratories worldwide.

*Task 2:*
Now run:

- `sudo systemctl stop ntp.service`
- `sudo ntpdate ntp.ubuntu.com`

(You can, of course, use a different time server in place of ntp.ubuntu.com.)

After a few seconds, you should see output indicating that `ntpdate` has updated the system time, noting where it got the time from and what the offset adjustment was.

`ntpdate` can be useful for updating the system time on every boot, sometimes before `ntpd` (the NTP daemon) takes over, or for synchronizing the time manually on servers that usually have restricted or no internet access. Beyond that, however, `ntpd` is recommended instead of running `ntpdate` via `cron`.

**Notes:**

`ntpq` is a command, mostly useful for debugging, that can be used to query NTP servers for various information.

# LAB 80

# Maintain System Time: Chrony

**Lab Objective:**
Learn how to maintain system time and synchronize the clock with Chrony.

**Lab Purpose:**
In this lab, you will learn about Chrony, a newer implementation of NTP, and its settings for synchronizing the system clock.

**Lab Tool:**
Ubuntu 18.04 (or another distro of your choice)

**Lab Topology:**
A single Linux machine, or virtual machine

**Lab Walkthrough:**

*Task 1:*
Open the Terminal and run:

- `sudo apt install chrony`
- `sudo systemctl start chrony`

Now view the main Chrony configuration file with: `cat /etc/chrony/chrony.conf`

You should recognize some similarities with the NTP config file from Lab 79.

*Task 2:*
Now run `sudo chronyc`. You will find yourself at an interactive prompt. You can now experiment with the `chronyc` tool:

- `tracking`
- `activity`
- `ntpdata`

Run `help` at this prompt to see a list of what you can do, or run `quit` to quit.

In comparison with `ntpd`, the chrony **FAQ page** states "If your computer is connected to the Internet only for a few minutes at a time, the network connection is often congested, you turn your computer off or suspend it frequently, the clock is not very stable (e.g. there are rapid changes in the temperature or it's a virtual machine), or you want to use NTP on an isolated network with no hardware reference clocks in sight, `chrony` will probably work much better for you."

**Notes:**

`hwclock` can be used to check the hardware time, which is not necessarily the same as system time (especially when the hardware clock uses a different timezone). Run `sudo hwclock` followed by `date`—do they match up?

The Chrony FAQ page URL is -

https://chrony.tuxfamily.org/faq.html#_how_does_code_chrony_code_compare_to_code_ntpd_code

# LAB 81

# System Logging: Rsyslog

**Lab Objective:**
Learn how to configure the `rsyslog` logging daemon.

**Lab Purpose:**
In this lab, you will learn about basic configuration of `rsyslog` and its different logging options.

**Lab Tool:**
Ubuntu 18.04 (or another distro of your choice)

**Lab Topology:**
A single Linux machine, or virtual machine

**Lab Walkthrough:**

*Task 1:*
Open two Terminal windows/tabs.

In the first one, run: `tail -f /var/log/syslog`

In the second one, run: `logger "Hello World"`

Now go back to the first tab. Did your friendly message show up in the system logs? Hit Ctrl+C to exit `tail`.

`logger` is a generic utility for sending logs to a number of daemons, including `rsyslog`, and `journald`, which we will discuss in Lab 83.

*Task 2:*
Now look at the configuration:

```
grep -v -e ^# -e ^$ /etc/rsyslog.conf /etc/rsyslog.d/*
```

This may vary by distro—once you locate the correct file(s), you may want to open them with a text editor.

Ultimately, you are looking for a file such as 50-default.conf or similar, defining what facilities log to what files. On Ubuntu, this file should contain a line like:

```
auth,authpriv.*                 /var/log/auth.log
```

At the top of this file, add the following line:

```
*.*                             /var/log/allthelogs
```

Then restart the daemon: `systemctl restart rsyslog`

Wait a few minutes (or create your own logs with `logger`), then check the contents of /var/log/allthelogs. This should be an amalgamation of all the logs which are going to many other log files.

### Task 3:
Clean up by deleting the line you added to the `rsyslog` config, and run `systemctl restart rsyslog`

**Notes:**

Aside from `journald`, which most distros have migrated to as a result of Systemd, there are also other logging daemons like `syslog` and `syslog-ng`. While some daemons have their own configuration formats, all at least support the classic syslog configuration format (and that should be what you saw in `rsyslog`'s own configs). Learn that format, and you will have learned configuration for all of the major logging daemons.

# LAB 82

## System Logging: Logrotate

**Lab Objective:**
Learn how to configure the `logrotate` to rotate system logs.

**Lab Purpose:**
`logrotate` is a commonly used tool to rotate logs, i.e. archive them every X days/weeks and delete them every Y weeks/months. In this lab, you will learn how to configure it.

**Lab Tool:**
Ubuntu 18.04 (or another distro of your choice)

**Lab Topology:**
A single Linux machine, or virtual machine

**Lab Walkthrough:**

*Task 1:*
Open the Terminal and run `cat /etc/logrotate.conf`

This is the main logrotate configuration file, the one that contains the default directives. You may see lines like:

```
weekly
rotate 4
create
```

In combination, these lines will save an archive of some log file every week, keep each archive for four weeks, and create a new empty log file after rotating an older one.

Additionally, you probably have a directory called /etc/logrotate.d, where some package-specific configs are stored. Ubuntu has one for `apt`, so look at /etc/logrotate.d/apt, or another file of your choosing.

You might see directives here like `rotate 12` (keep for 12 weeks instead of 4, or 12 months if it includes `monthly`), `compress` to compress the archives, or `notifempty` to ignore the log if it is empty.

See `man logrotate` for more details.

*Task 2:*
Now, with `sudo` (or `sudoedit`), open a text editor and create a file called /etc/logrotate.d/mylog with the following contents:

```
/var/log/mylog.log {
  hourly
  su root syslog
  rotate 2
  create
  compress
  missingok
}
```

Then: `sudo touch /var/log/mylog.log`

Normally you'd have to wait at least an hour to see any rotation happen, but you can force the situation with the `-f` switch. Run:

- `sudo logrotate -fv /etc/logrotate.d/mylog`
- `ls -al /var/log/mylog*`

You should see a compressed archive of the original file, as mylog.log.1.gz, and a new log called mylog.log. Run that first command twice more. The second time you run it will create a second archive file, but on the third run you should see a line at the bottom saying "removing old log /var/log/mylog.log.3.gz", as per the configuration file.

*Task 3:*
Finally, clean up: `sudo rm /etc/logrotate.d/mylog /var/log/mylog*`

**Notes:**
Typically, `logrotate` is run via a daily cron job. Can you find where this cron job is configured on your system? (Hint: See Lab 75!)

# LAB 83

# System Logging: Journald

**Lab Objective:**
Learn how to manage and read data from `journald`, the Systemd logger.

**Lab Purpose:**
In this lab, you will get to know `journald`, the Systemd logging system that is slowly replacing classic `syslog` variants in most Linux distros.

**Lab Tool:**
Ubuntu 18.04 (or another distro of your choice)

**Lab Topology:**
A single Linux machine, or virtual machine

**Lab Walkthrough:**

*Task 1:*
Open two Terminal windows/tabs.

In the first one, run: `journalctl -f`

In the second one, run: `systemd-cat echo "Hello World"`

Now go back to the first tab. Did your friendly message show up in the system logs? Hit Ctrl+C to exit.

`systemd-cat` is a convenient tool, like `logger`, that can send output directly to the `journald` logs.

*Task 2:*
Now look at the configuration: `cat /etc/systemd/journald.conf`

On a default Ubuntu 18.04 system, you will probably see... a lot of commented-out lines. This is just the default configuration, which can still tell you a lot. You can learn the meaning of these options from `man journald.conf`, which is conveniently laid out in the same order as the config file.

Use the two tabs from Task 1, or open a second tab if necessary. In the first tab, run `tty`, then save the value it prints out for later.

In the second tab, open /etc/systemd/journald.conf for editing as root (via `sudo` or `sudoedit`). Append these two lines to the bottom of the file:

```
ForwardToConsole=yes
TTYPath=[tty]
```

... where `[tty]` is the value printed by `tty` in the other tab. Save and quit the editor, then run:

- `sudo systemctl restart systemd-journald`
- `systemd-cat echo "Hello World"`

Now look back at the first tab again. You should see logs being printed directly to your console! This can be useful for monitoring system logs, generally, without having to keep a process running.

*Task 3:*
Clean up:

- Edit /etc/systemd/journald.conf again and delete the two lines you added
- Run `sudo systemctl restart systemd-journald`

**Notes:**
When stored persistently on the disk (which is typically what you want to do, as opposed to only storing logs in memory), `journald` logs are stored in /var/log/journal. If you try to read these files, however, you will quickly notice that they are not the text logs you may be used to! Somewhat inconveniently, `journald` stores its logs in a binary format which is only readable by systemd-related tools.

# LAB 84

## Mail Transfer Agent (MTA) Basics: Aliases and Forwarding

**Lab Objective:**
Learn how to perform basic mail forwarding and alias configuration.

**Lab Purpose:**
In this lab, you will experiment with the Postfix MTA to learn about aliases and mail forwarding.

**Lab Tool:**
Ubuntu 18.04 (or another distro of your choice)

**Lab Topology:**
A single Linux machine, or virtual machine

**Lab Walkthrough:**

*Task 1:*
First, install Postfix: `sudo apt install postfix mailutils`

On Ubuntu, you will be prompted to ask how you want to configure Postfix initially. Choose the "Local only" option, and leave any other options as the default.

You've set up a mail server that is meant only to deliver messages to other local users. This means that in the rest of this lab, where you might normally see an e-mail address (formatted@likethis.com), you will see only a username.

*Task 2:*
Now run `cat /etc/aliases`

This is a system-wide alias list for the purpose of mail redirection. Right now the file probably only has one line, which tells Postfix that mail to 'postmaster' should go to root.

Add your own alias:

- `sudo USER=$USER sh -c 'echo "mymail: $USER" >> /etc/aliases'`
- `sudo newaliases`

The aliases are stored in a database, which `newaliases` refreshes. Now you can send a message to the 'mymail' user and have it forwarded to you: `echo "Hello World" | sendmail mymail`

You might be wondering what `sendmail` is doing there. Sendmail was one of the first Linux MTA's, woven into the early fabric of the internet—but that is not the MTA you installed above. Because Sendmail was so central to e-mail on Linux for many years, most major open-source MTA's, including Postfix, have an emulation layer for it.

*Task 3:*
Now, confirm that you received the message sent to 'mymail':

- Run: `mail`
- You will see your inbox, in text format. Ideally, the message you sent is the first one, but it doesn't really matter. Enter 1 to read the first message in your inbox (including the headers, which you might not normally see—don't be thrown off by this).
- When you're done, enter q to quit.

*Task 4:*
In addition to system-wide mail forwarding, a user can control their own mail forwarding by adding a .forward file to their home directory. Try it yourself:

- `echo root > ~/.forward`
- `echo "Forwarding enabled" | mail -s "A forwarded message" mymail`
- `mail`
- `sudo mail`

If you did it correctly, the first `mail` command should print "No mail for [username]", or at least show an inbox without the message you just sent. root's inbox should show the message instead.

## Lab 84–Mail Transfer Agent (MTA) Basics: Aliases and Forwarding

*Task 5:*

Finally, clean up:

- `rm ~/.forward`
- `sudo sed -i '/mymail:/d' /etc/aliases`
- `sudo newaliases`

**Notes:**

You might find the `mail` command's inbox a bit hard to navigate. This is, of course, why people install and use their own mail clients. Even on the Linux command line, you would typically use something like `mutt` or `alpine`.

# LAB 85

## Mail Transfer Agent (MTA) Basics: Other MTA's

**Lab Objective:**
Learn about other major MTA's, like Sendmail and Exim.

**Lab Purpose:**
In this lab, you will experiment with MTA's other than Postfix (which was featured in Lab 84).

**Lab Tool:**
Ubuntu 18.04 (or another distro of your choice)

**Lab Topology:**
A single Linux machine, or virtual machine

**Lab Walkthrough:**

*Task 1:*
First, install Exim: `sudo apt install exim4`

Like Postfix, Exim also has an emulation layer for the classic Sendmail. If you check the man pages for commands like `newaliases` or `mailq`, you will instead see the man page for `exim4`.

You can do all of the things with Exim that you did in Lab 84, including aliases and sending mail with `sendmail`. (The `mail` command is actually part of a different package, `mailutils`.)

*Task 2:*
Now, install the venerable Sendmail: `sudo apt install sendmail-bin sendmail`

This is the classic MTA, so it doesn't have an emulation layer... though it may feel like it does, just because of how long some commands can take. (Compare the run time, for instance, of `newaliases` under Sendmail vs. under Postfix.)

Again, however, all of the old commands from the previous lab should be familiar to you, and should work in familiar ways.

*Task 3:*

Finally, take the most important step you will take in this lab, by removing Sendmail. Sendmail has a well-deserved reputation for security problems, so even on a lab machine, it's best not to keep around longer than necessary:

- `sudo apt remove sendmail-bin sendmail`
- `sudo apt autoremove`

**Notes:**

Another thing you can do with aliases is forward mail to a file, rather than another user. However, Exim doesn't allow this by default—you'd have to wade into the configurations to do so.

# LAB 86

## Manage Printers and Printing

**Lab Objective:**
Learn how to manage print jobs using CUPS.

**Lab Purpose:**
In this lab, you will learn about managing print queues and jobs using CUPS and the LPD compatibility interface.

**Lab Tool:**
Ubuntu 18.04 (or another distro of your choice)

**Lab Topology:**
A single Linux machine, or virtual machine

**Lab Walkthrough:**

*Task 1:*
To eliminate variability around printer hardware and all the problems it brings (and in case you don't have a printer handy), this lab will assume printing to a PDF file instead. If you would like to print to a real printer, ignore this step. Otherwise, run: `sudo apt install printer-driver-cups-pdf` (you may have to run 'apt-get update --fix-missing' in order to install cups-pdf correctly.

Verify with `lpstat -t`—you should see "device for PDF: cups-pdf:/" as part of the output. Or, if you plug in a real printer, it should be auto-detected. (If not, then it would be easier to print to PDF for the purposes of this lab.)

Finally, check where your files should be printed: `grep ^Out /etc/cups/cups-pdf.conf`

You may see something like ${HOME}/PDF as the directory where your "printed" files will end up. You can change this if you like; if you do, finalize it with `sudo systemctl restart cups`

## Task 2:
You can probably guess what happens next:

- `echo "Hello World" | lpr`
- Locate the file in the directory you identified above (it may have an odd name, like stdin___tu_PDF-job_1.pdf), and open it in a PDF viewer or web browser.

You should find a nondescript PDF file with your text printed in the top left corner. If you didn't change anything, this should be under PDF/ in your home directory.

## Task 3:
Now some other helpful commands:

- `lpr -T gibberish`
- Type some gibberish, followed by Ctrl+C to cancel. (The `-T` flag also influences the filename after printing.)
- `lpq`
- The previous command should tell you the job number (third column) of the queued job. Then run: `lprm [number]`
- You canceled the job (if you do it quickly enough—there is a timeout), but it will still show up as "completed" via `lpstat -W completed`

**Notes:**
`lpadmin` can be used to add and configure printers which are not auto-detected. For example, you would add a cups-pdf printer manually with:

```
sudo lpadmin -p cups-pdf -v cups-pdf:/ -E -P /usr/share/ppd/cups-pdf/
CUPS-PDF_opt.ppd
```

# LAB 87

# Fundamentals of Internet Protocols: Ports and Services

**Lab Objective:**
Learn how to gather information on ports and services on a Linux system.

**Lab Purpose:**
In this lab, you will examine some common networking principles, namely ports and services, using some Linux command-line tools.

**Lab Tool:**
Ubuntu 18.04 (or another distro of your choice)

**Lab Topology:**
A single Linux machine, or virtual machine

**Lab Walkthrough:**

*Task 1:*
Open the terminal and run: `sudo ss -Saputn`

This is a list of currently open connections and listening ports on your machine. There's a lot of output here, but you're mostly interested in the first column and the last three columns.

The first column lists what protocol each connection follows. Most likely this will be either UDP or TCP, which you may recall are faster/connectionless and more-reliable/connection-oriented, respectively.

Columns 5 and 6 list your IP:port and the remote host's IP:port. Lab 89 will discuss IP addressing, but you're interested in the port numbers here. TCP and UDP each have 65,535 ports available, some of which are assigned (either officially, by IANA, or unofficially by common use) to various services.

Look at the port numbers and try to identify which services are using each "server" port. The server port is important, because the client port (the port from which a client first makes a connection) is usually dynamic. It may help to look at column 7 to see what process on your machine is using the connection.

*Task 2:*
Programs commonly use the /etc/services file to map service names to the port(s) they should listen or connect on. The file is human-readable, however, so you should look yourself.

By looking through /etc/services (with `cat /etc/services`), can you identify what services your machine was listening for, or connecting to, in Task 1? Can you identify which ports are used by common services, such as HTTP, SSH, LDAP, SNMP, and SMTP?

*Task 3:*
Another very common protocol is one that you won't find any listening ports for... because it doesn't have ports! This is ICMP, a.k.a. "ping" (though in reality, it is used for much more than pinging).

Open two terminal windows/tabs. In the first one, run: `sudo tcpdump -n -i any icmp`

In the second one, run: `ping -c 5 localhost`

Go back to the first tab, and you should see the requests and replies from your pings—and maybe some other ICMP traffic too, if you're lucky.

**Notes:**
If you couldn't see any traffic or get any ICMP replies in the last task, a firewall on your machine may be to blame. Blocking ICMP traffic indiscriminately like that is a poor practice, so it's an exercise to the student to figure out how to open that up a little. (Hint: `iptables`)

# LAB 88

## Fundamentals of Internet Protocols: Subnetting

**Lab Objective:**
Learn how to gather information on subnets on a Linux system.

**Lab Purpose:**
In this lab, you will examine some common networking principles, namely subnetting, using some Linux command-line tools.

**Lab Tool:**
Ubuntu 18.04 (or another distro of your choice)

**Lab Topology:**
A single Linux machine, or virtual machine

**Lab Walkthrough:**

*Task 1:*
An IP subnetting tutorial is outside the scope of this lab, but if you have done a lot of it, you may have wished for a tool to help you with the math (maybe you even have one already). Well, Linux has one!

Run: `sudo apt install sipcalc`

To use `sipcalc`, you'll first want to know your own IP address(es). Get these with: `ip addr show`

This command prints a tree of sorts, with each network interface being a "root". You probably have at least two interfaces, a localhost interface named 'lo' and an Ethernet interface (or Wi-Fi on a laptop non-VM) named 'enp0s3' or something similar. Below that, you're looking for the lines beginning with 'inet' and 'inet6'—those are your IP addresses.

You can put those into `sipcalc` and get information like the network mask, broadcast address, and usable network range:

```
sipcalc 127.0.0.1/8
```

It also works with IPv6 addresses.

**Notes:**
There's a more colorful alternative to `sipcalc`, called `ipcalc`. `ipcalc`, however, does not support IPv6.

# LAB 89

# Fundamentals of Internet Protocols: IPv4 and IPv6

**Lab Objective:**
Learn how to gather information about IP addressing on a Linux system.

**Lab Purpose:**
In this lab, you will examine some common networking principles, namely IPv4, IPv6, and the differences between them, using some Linux command-line tools.

**Lab Tool:**
Ubuntu 18.04 (or another distro of your choice)

**Lab Topology:**
A single Linux machine, or virtual machine

**Lab Walkthrough:**

*Task 1:*
In Lab 88, you installed `sipcalc` and used it to gather information on your machine's IP addresses. Now you will use the same tool, but examine its output more closely and compare it with other configurations on your system.

Your system should have at least two IP addresses, one private IPv4 and one link-local IPv6. You may not have both an IPv4 and IPv6 public address, so this lab will use the private ones. Get those as discussed in Lab 88 with: `ip addr show`

Compare the output of:

- `sipcalc -a [IPv4]`
- `sipcalc -a [IPv6]`

You may be aware that IPv4 and IPv6 have quite a few differences, but even the subnetting output reflects that.

There are subtle differences, too, when it comes to system administration that you may not be aware of. For example, run this exercise as you did in Lab 87:

- Open two terminal windows/tabs
- In the first, run: `sudo tcpdump -n -i any icmp`
- In the second, run: `ping6 -c 5 ip6-localhost`

If all goes well, you should see the ping replies. But what happens when you check back to the first tab? Where are the ICMP packets?

The answer, as you may have discovered, is to use 'icmp6' instead of 'icmp'. But even that isn't universal—`ip6tables` (the IPv6 version of `iptables`) calls it 'ipv6-icmp'... despite the fact that `ip6tables` only operates on IPv6 traffic anyway.

In short: When in doubt, read the man pages.

**Notes:**
There's a more colorful alternative to `sipcalc`, called `ipcalc`. `ipcalc`, however, does not support Ipv6.

# LAB 90

## Persistent Network Configuration: Network Configuration

**Lab Objective:**
Learn how to configure networking on a Linux host.

**Lab Purpose:**
In this lab, you will learn how to configure a Linux host as a network client, using various files and tools.

**Lab Tool:**
Ubuntu 18.04 (or another distro of your choice)

**Lab Topology:**
A single Linux machine, or virtual machine

**Lab Walkthrough:**

*Task 1:*
Open the Terminal and use `cat`, or your favorite text editor, to view the contents of the following files:

- /etc/hostname
- /etc/hosts
- /etc/resolv.conf
- /etc/nsswitch.conf

It is likely that management of these files has been swallowed up by Systemd, but it is nonetheless important to understand what each of them does (or did).

They're listed in order of decreasing simplicity. /etc/hostname simply lists your machine's hostname—in practice, to *change* the hostname, you would use `hostname` or `hostnamectl`.

/etc/hosts was DNS before DNS existed. It is a mapping of hostnames to IP addresses, useful for local addresses, small networks, and sometimes DNS servers may go here as well.

/etc/resolv.conf lists the IP addresses of your DNS servers, and possibly some other related options. (As mentioned in the file comments, this has now been taken over by `systemd-resolved`.)

/etc/nsswitch.conf is a bit outside the scope of this lab, but the relevant lines here are the ones starting with 'hosts:' and 'networks:'. The next word on those lines should be 'files', which just means that certain applications will consult the files you've just viewed when seeking that information. You may make significant edits to nsswitch.conf if you connect to centralized authentication, e.g. when an LDAP server should be queried for information rather than /etc/passwd.

*Task 2:*
You've worked with `ip` in previous labs to get network information, but it's worth reiterating. It is a powerful tool with a lot of uses:

- `ip address`
- `ip maddress`
- `ip route`
- `ip netconf`

**Notes:**
In the next lab, you will learn how to change the current IP settings, using NetworkManager.

# LAB 91

# Persistent Network Configuration: NetworkManager

**Lab Objective:**
Learn how to configure TCP/IP on a Linux host using NetworkManager.

**Lab Purpose:**
In this lab, you will learn how to configure a Linux host as a network client, using NetworkManager.

**Lab Tool:**
Ubuntu 18.04 (or another distro of your choice)

**Lab Topology:**
A single Linux machine, or virtual machine

**Lab Walkthrough:**

*Task 1:*
While you may have familiarized yourself with NetworkManager as a GUI tool, this lab will focus on the command-line version, `nmcli`.

Open the Terminal and get a nice view of your networking information, all in one place: `nmcli`

Presumably, your network connection is working right now… so let's break it:

    nmcli n off

All this did was take the overall networking control and shut it off. Simplistic, but effective. Turn it back on with: `nmcli n on`

You can also disable an individual link, Wi-Fi radio, etc. But now focus on modifying values. First, get the right device: `nmcli d`

You should have a device that is connected on a wired or wireless connection; get that device name from the first column and use it below:

```
nmcli d show [device]
```

Now grab your IP address and gateway from the second column and save those for later.

### Task 2:
Now modify your IP settings:

```
nmcli d mod [device] ipv4.method manual ipv4.address [address/netmask]
ipv4.gateway [gateway]
```

Ideally, you should choose values for [address/netmask] and [gateway] that are different from what you already had, but just slightly. Your network will almost certainly break if you change both values (test it yourself).

If you want, you can use nmcli again to restore the previous values; the command will differ depending on whether you were using DHCP or not. However, the simplest and most foolproof way to fix your connection is to do what you did earlier... the classic "turn it off and back on again":

- nmcli n off
- nmcli n on

**Notes:**
Another great tool for managing network configurations is netplan. This is less useful for clients, and more useful on servers with more complex setups.

# LAB 92

## Basic Network Troubleshooting: Modern Tools

**Lab Objective:**
Learn how to troubleshoot networking issues on Linux with `iproute2`.

**Lab Purpose:**
In this lab, you will experiment with the latest Linux networking tools, some of which are part of the `iproute2` package.

**Lab Tool:**
Ubuntu 18.04 (or another distro of your choice)

**Lab Topology:**
A single Linux machine, or virtual machine. IPv6 must be enabled within virtual your lab for those tools to work, otherwise all steps will return a 'network is unreachable' error.

**Lab Walkthrough:**

*Task 1:*
Open your Terminal and run the following commands to gather information on your current network configuration:

- `ip addr show`
- `ip route show`
- `ss -ap`
- `hostname -f`
- `nmcli`

*Task 2:*

Install traceroute: `sudo apt install traceroute`

Now run a few more commands to verify that you have end-to-end connectivity with **101labs.net**, and trace the routes in between.

- `ping 101labs.net`
- `traceroute 101labs.net`
- `sudo traceroute -I 101labs.net`
- `tracepath -b 101labs.net`

The first `traceroute` and `tracepath` commands here are using UDP, while the second `traceroute` is using ICMP. Sometimes the methods will yield different results; sometimes not.

If you have IPv6 connectivity, you can also experiment with those versions of the tools. (At the time of this writing, 101labs.net does not have an IPv6 address.)

- `ping6 example.com`
- `traceroute6 example.com`
- `tracepath6 -b example.com`

**Notes:**

For any kind of non-trivial network troubleshooting, `netcat` is a useful tool to know. It can act as an arbitrary client or server for TCP, UDP, or UNIX-domain sockets, and supports IPv4 and IPv6.

# LAB 93

## Basic Network Troubleshooting: Legacy Tools

**Lab Objective:**
Learn how to troubleshoot networking issues on Linux with `net-tools`.

**Lab Purpose:**
In this lab, you will experiment with some classic Linux networking tools which are part of the `net-tools` package.

**Lab Tool:**
Ubuntu 18.04 (or another distro of your choice)

**Lab Topology:**
A single Linux machine, or virtual machine

**Lab Walkthrough:**

*Task 1:*
First, install the net-tools package if you don't already have it:

```
sudo apt install net-tools
```

Now run the following commands to gather information on your current network configuration:

- `ifconfig -a -v`
- `sudo netstat -tulnp`
- `route -v`
- `ipmaddr show`
- `arp -ve`

Since these tools are deprecated, it is best to uninstall them when finished: `sudo apt remove net-tools`

**Notes:**

The `net-tools` package has not been actively updated for about a decade. Though change is slow and it is still available in most package repos, it is clear at this point that `ifconfig` and its ilk won't be coming back. `ipmaddr` has been replaced by `ip maddress`.

# LAB 94

# Configure Client-Side DNS: dnsutils

**Lab Objective:**
Learn how to use classic Linux utilities to configure client-side DNS.

**Lab Purpose:**
In this lab you will work with classic tools such as `dig` to configure and troubleshoot DNS resolution.

**Lab Tool:**
Ubuntu 18.04 (or another distro of your choice)

**Lab Topology:**
A single Linux machine, or virtual machine

**Lab Walkthrough:**

*Task 1:*
In ye olden days, one could just `cat /etc/hosts /etc/resolv.conf` and gather all the DNS information one needed. This is, sadly, no longer true. Instead, run `nmcli` to find out what your current DNS servers are (see "DNS configuration" near the bottom), then save these for later. You probably have two nameservers, which will be referred to as `[dns1]` and `[dns2]` below.

*Task 2:*
Now you will experiment with `dig`, one of the most common and useful DNS troubleshooting utilities:

- `dig 101labs.net`
- `dig 101labs.net MX +short`
- `dig CNAME www.101labs.net [dns1]`
- `dig AAAA example.com [dns2] +short`

There are many more options available, most of which you will probably never need—but, as always, the man page is worth a skim.

*Task 3:*
Not to be outdone, `host` can do many of the same things that `dig` can:

- `host -v -t A 101labs.net`
- `host -t MX 101labs.net`
- `host -v -t CNAME www.101labs.net [dns1]`
- `host -t AAAA example.com [dns2]`

See the similarities?

*Task 4:*
By default, Ubuntu 18.04 uses a local caching nameserver. If you run a non-recursive query on this (with the dig option `+norecurse`), it will come up empty:

`dig 101labs.net +norecurse 127.0.0.53`

Run this on one of your main nameservers and it will work.

**Notes:**
`resolvconf` is a tool that was previously used in Ubuntu to manage resolv.conf. No longer installed by default, it seems to have been superseded by `systemd-resolved`.

For some users, the dig and host commands for the AAAA record required 'www' before the "example" address.

# LAB 95

## Configure Client-Side DNS: systemd-resolved

**Lab Objective:**
Learn how to use Systemd utilities to configure client-side DNS.

**Lab Purpose:**
In this lab you will work with Systemd to configure and troubleshoot DNS resolution.

**Lab Tool:**
Ubuntu 18.04 (or another distro of your choice)

**Lab Topology:**
A single Linux machine, or virtual machine

**Lab Walkthrough:**

*Task 1:*
Open the Terminal and run: `systemd-resolve --status`

This is another, Systemd-friendly way of getting your DNS servers, along with some other information. Hold onto those nameserver addresses for below.

Most likely your DNS servers will be listed as local, under your main network interface, rather than global. You can edit the global nameservers this way:

- Add a line like `DNS=1.2.3.4 5.6.7.8` to /etc/systemd/resolved.conf
- Run: `sudo systemctl restart systemd-resolved`

But in this case, you can also just change the DNS servers attached to the current interface (which you should identify the name of above, e.g. enp0s3):

```
systemd-resolve --set-dns=1.2.3.4 --set-dns=5.6.7.8
--interface=[interface]
```

Now, if you type that command as-is, your DNS will break, because, of course, those addresses aren't real DNS servers. You can substitute the IP addresses for real public nameservers if you like.

In either case, you'll probably want to switch back to what you had before:

```
systemd-resolve --set-dns=[dns1] --set-dns=[dns2]
--interface=[interface]
```

**Notes:**

`systemd-resolve` can also be used to make DNS queries a la `dig`, but its options for this are much more limited.

# LAB 96

## Perform Security Administration Tasks: User Auditing

**Lab Objective:**
Learn how to manage and audit users and user restrictions.

**Lab Purpose:**
In this lab, you will review a variety of tools used to manage users and maintain security through limitations on their privileges.

**Lab Tool:**
Ubuntu 18.04 (or another distro of your choice)

**Lab Topology:**
A single Linux machine, or virtual machine

**Lab Walkthrough:**

*Task 1:*
Throughout most of these labs, you've used `sudo` to grant yourself root privileges for certain tasks. Now, it's finally time to learn how to configure it:

- `sudo useradd luser`
- `sudo visudo`
- Under the "User privilege specification", add the following line:
  `luser        ALL=NOPASSWD:/usr/sbin/useradd`
- `sudo su luser`
- `sudo useradd luser2`
- `exit`

In this sequence, you edited the /etc/sudoers configuration file safely with `visudo` (which you should always do—a syntax error in the sudoers file can lock you out of your own system!) The addition means that the 'luser' user can run `useradd` as root, without being prompted for a password. "ALL" here means that it can be run on "ALL" systems, which in this case is only one, since you aren't connected to a NIS domain.

After switching to luser, you should have been able to add another user seamlessly, without being prompted. If you tried any other `sudo` command, you would be prompted for a password and the command would fail altogether.

## Task 2:
Now run (the first command should all be on one line):

- `sudo sh -c 'echo "luser hard nproc 2" >> /etc/security/limits.conf'`
- `sudo su luser`
- `ulimit -a`
- `sleep 10000 &`
- `sleep 10000 &`
- `exit`

Attempting to run the second `sleep`, you should have been greeted with a mysterious error about "Cannot fork". What's going on here? Your first command applied a limit of 2 user processes to the 'luser' user. The shell counts as one process, which means luser can't do a whole lot after that! This is why the first `sleep` was successful while the second one failed.

Remove the process limit from luser in /etc/security/limits.conf before moving on.

## Task 3:
Now, a few commands to audit user activity and logins:

- `who -a`
- `w`
- `lastlog`

## Task 4:
Finally, clean up:

- Run `sudo visudo` and delete the 'luser' line that you added
- `sudo userdel luser`
- `sudo userdel luser2`

**Notes:**
See Lab 74 for more information on how to restrict user password validity and other similar features. If you are unable to delete user "luser" at the end of the lab, because the user is still used by a process, you can find the PID being called to kill. luser needs to log out before deletion.

# LAB 97

## Perform Security Administration Tasks: System Auditing

**Lab Objective:**
Learn how to manage and audit ports, processes, and other system aspects.

**Lab Purpose:**
In this lab, you will review a variety of tools used to manage services, ports, file permissions, and other features to maintain a secure Linux system.

**Lab Tool:**
Ubuntu 18.04 (or another distro of your choice)

**Lab Topology:**
A single Linux machine, or virtual machine

**Lab Walkthrough:**

*Task 1:*
Open the Terminal and run:

```
sudo find / -perm /u=s,g=s -type f -exec ls -l {} \; 2>/dev/null
```

That's a hairy command, so let's break it down. Here, you're finding all files on the system with either the setuid or setgid bits set (or both), which are regular files (and not directories or some other special file). Then you execute `ls -l` on each of those files. The `2>/dev/null` is just to silence some spurious errors about special filesystems like /proc.

The end result should be a detailed list of possibly "insecure" files on your system—files which are run with their owner and/or group permissions instead of the permissions of the user who executed them.

## LPIC1 LINUX ADMINISTRATOR–EXAM 102

*Task 2:*

In previous labs, you've used `ss` to list open ports. However, there are other approaches. Install the `nmap` port scanner: `sudo apt install nmap`

Now run a standard `nmap` scan: `sudo nmap -v -sU -sS -p1-65535 localhost`

This command may take quite some time. It will run a standard UDP and TCP SYN scan of every port on your system. An `nmap` scan, when run from a remote host (which you did not do here), is a great way to get a look at open ports on your system from an outside perspective.

**Notes:**

`fuser` and `lsof` are two tools which can be used to link files and processes, but they work differently. `fuser` is handier to answer the question of "Which process opened this file?", while `lsof` would be better to answer "Which files did this process open?"

# LAB 98

# Setup Host Security: User Security

**Lab Objective:**
Learn how to use login-related features to secure a Linux host.

**Lab Purpose:**
In this lab you will review shadow passwords and login restriction features to secure a Linux host.

**Lab Tool:**
Ubuntu 18.04 (or another distro of your choice)

**Lab Topology:**
A single Linux machine, or virtual machine

**Lab Walkthrough:**

*Task 1:*
We've discussed the /etc/shadow file in previous labs, but now we're going to take a closer look at it. The second field in a given shadow file entry is the password, obfuscated by a one-way hashing algorithm. Most users are probably system users and thus don't have passwords, but at least your user should.

Take a look at `man 3 crypt`—this is how those hashes are created. The man page notes that a hash is split into 3 sections, delimited by dollar signs. The first is an ID denoting the encryption method. Look at your shadow hash again—what is the ID number in the first field? If it's a 6, then your password is hashed with SHA-512 and you're in good shape. If it's a 5, your hash is SHA-256—not the best, but still pretty good. A password hash beginning with a 1 is MD5, and only likely if the hash was copied from an older system. (If you have any hashes like that, you should run `passwd` for those users to change them.)

## Task 2:
Now run: `man 5 nologin`

The /etc/nologin file, which disallows non-root logins and shows those users a message of whatever is in the file, is great for putting a system into emergency maintenance. Aside from that, you probably don't want it to be present!

**Notes:**
`cracklib` is a password-cracking library that can be used with tools like `shadow` and PAM to enforce secure password practices.

# LAB 99

## Setup Host Security: Network Services

**Lab Objective:**
Learn how to restrict network services on a Linux host.

**Lab Purpose:**
In this lab you will learn how to securely configure and turn off unused network services.

**Lab Tool:**
Ubuntu 18.04 (or another distro of your choice)

**Lab Topology:**
A single Linux machine, or virtual machine

**Lab Walkthrough:**

*Task 1:*
Install xinetd: `sudo apt install xinetd`

`xinetd` is a general network services daemon, or "super-server"; it listens on multiple ports and then filters the connections and launches a listener for the relevant service when needed.

Take a look at some of the default configurations, like /etc/xinetd.d/echo. These are internal services and disabled by default; you may find some of the man page examples helpful, in terms of illustrating how you can use `xinetd` to run arbitrary servers (out of shell scripts, etc.)

*Task 2:*
Are your `ss` and `nmap` outputs not as clean as they could be? Do you still have an orphaned mail server running from Lab 85? Now you'll look for and shut down some of these unnecessary services.

Let's say that in your output from `ss -aptu`, you have a sendmail-mta process running that shouldn't be there. (You should run the command and pick an unnecessary service for yourself.)

There are no right answers here because the steps depend greatly upon your system and your services, but here are some general guidelines to follow:

- What is the status of the Systemd service, if it exists (`sudo systemctl status` _____)?
- Have you uninstalled the relevant package(s) via the package manager? If so, run `sudo updatedb && sudo locate` _____—an incomplete removal could leave files behind.
- Once the files are gone, you can kill the process with `kill -9 [pid]`
- If you want to keep the service but not have it start automatically, try: `sudo systemctl disable` _____

**Notes:**

A `systemd.socket` unit is analogous to xinetd, particularly with Accept=True in its configuration. Systemd sockets are meant to listen on network sockets in lieu of more resource-intensive services, until those services are actually needed. `xinetd` is still in common use, so Systemd sockets haven't quite superseded it.

# LAB 100

# Securing Data with Encryption: SSH

**Lab Objective:**
Learn how to operate OpenSSH to create a secure network tunnel.

**Lab Purpose:**
In this lab, you will learn about OpenSSH, a common tool for creating secure connections and tunnels to/from Linux servers.

**Lab Tool:**
Ubuntu 18.04 (or another distro of your choice)

**Lab Topology:**
A single Linux machine, or virtual machine

**Lab Walkthrough:**

*Task 1:*
First, install openssh-server: `sudo apt install openssh-server`

Now run: `ssh-keygen -t ed25519`

You can save your user's SSH key in the default location, but make sure to choose a password—you will use this later.

Copy the public key into authorized_keys to allow yourself SSH access: `cp .ssh/id_ed25519.pub .ssh/authorized_keys`

Finally, get your machine's host keys:

```
ssh-keyscan localhost | ssh-keygen -lf -
```

Save the bottom three lines somewhere; those are your host key fingerprints, in different formats, and you will use one of them later.

## LPIC1 Linux Administrator—Exam 102

*Task 2:*
Now run:

- `eval $(ssh-agent)`
- `ssh-add`
- Type your password. This will cache your SSH private key to `ssh-agent` so you don't have to type the password again during this session (while maintaining its security).

Finally, connect with SSH: `ssh localhost`

You should be prompted to confirm a previously unknown host key. Compare this key with the three host keys you saved from Task 1; one of them should be a match. (If not, something has gone wrong.) Assuming so, confirm the connection and you should now be connected locally over SSH, without having to type your password again.

*Task 3:*
Run `exit`, then run `ssh localhost` again just to be sure you can connect with no prompts. Now run:

- `exit`
- `kill $SSH_AGENT_PID`
- `ssh localhost`

Did you have to type your password this time to unlock your key?

**Notes:**
Make sure you can follow and understand all the steps that are happening in this fairly complex process:

- Installing the OpenSSH server. This step generates host keys automatically.
- Generating a keypair for your user, and granting yourself access by creating an authorized_keys file containing the public key.
- Getting the server's host key fingerprints for later verification.
- Initializing the `ssh-agent` caching tool and adding your private key to it.
- Connecting over SSH (even if to localhost), verifying the host key, and permanently saving the fingerprint.

# LAB 101

# Securing Data with Encryption: GPG

**Lab Objective:**
Learn how to operate GPG for data encryption and verification.

**Lab Purpose:**
In this lab, you will learn about GnuPG, a tool used to encrypt, decrypt, sign, and verify data of files, e-mails, and package updates, among other things.

**Lab Tool:**
Ubuntu 18.04 (or another distro of your choice)

**Lab Topology:**
A single Linux machine, or virtual machine

**Lab Walkthrough:**

*Task 1:*
Open the Terminal and run: `gpg --generate-key`

You will be prompted for a name and e-mail address, then GPG will do the rest. Afterwards, run `gpg --generate-key` again to create a second key for a different fictitious person.

List the keys you created with `gpg -k`

Finally, take a peek at ~/.gnupg. In this directory, you should see a trust database (trustdb.gpg) and public keyring (pubring.kbx), as well as an openpgp-revocs.d directory for revocation certificates, and private-keys-v1.d directory containing your private key files.

*Task 2:*
Now let's try sending a secret message between your two imaginary GPG users:

- `echo "Hello World" > secret`
- `gpg -se -r [email2] secret`
- `file secret.gpg`
- `gpg -d < secret.gpg`

In this scenario, a file has been sent from [email1] to [email2]. You signed and then encrypted the file with the second user's public key; secret.gpg was the result, which, as `file` should tell you, is a PGP RSA encrypted session key. Finally, you decrypt this file and are shown an encryption header, and the message itself, followed by a signature (which GPG informs you is good).

**Notes:**

In a real-world scenario, you would be importing keys either from a third-party directly or from a public keyserver, and then assigning them trust values. "Trust" in GPG-speak means "How much do you trust this person to properly verify someone else's key before signing it?" Recommended research: the web of trust.

CPSIA information can be obtained
at www.ICGtesting.com
Printed in the USA
LVHW101524040220
645815LV00006B/256